KEYS TO LIVING
WITH A
RETIRED HUSBAND

Gloria Bledsoe Goodman

All inquiries should be addressed to:
Barron's Educational Series, Inc.
250 Wireless Boulevard
Hauppauge, New York 11788

Library of Congress Catalog Card No. 91-15493

International Standard Book No. 0-8120-4705-2

Library of Congress Cataloging-in-Publication Data

Goodman, Gloria Bledsoe.
    Keys to living with a retired husband / by Gloria Bledsoe Goodman.
        p.   cm.—(Barron's retirement keys)
    Includes index.
    ISBN 0-8120-4705-2
    1. Retirement—United States.   2. Husbands—United States.
    3. Retirees—United States—Psychology.   4. Retirees—United States—
    Life skills guides.   I. Title.   II. Series.
    HQ1063.2.U6G66   1991
    646.7'9—dc20   91-15493
                                                                CIP

PRINTED IN THE UNITED STATES OF AMERICA
1234   5500   987654321

CONTENTS

INTRODUCTION

The retirement celebration is over, and now you and your mate are ready to settle down to the rest of your life together. As a wife, whether employed or a home-maker, you are no doubt wondering about the coming years and what changes lie ahead.

One of the first things you must do is to stop and really evaluate your feelings about living with a full-time husband. Are you approaching this new lifestyle with dread? With trepidation? With apprehension? Relax. The fear of the unknown is quite common, but it should never paralyze the way in which you move toward new experiences.

Look upon your husband's retirement as a period of pluses. As a reward for your busy work years, you two will be able to:

—Enjoy leisure time to pursue whatever activity appeals to you as a couple. Sports, travel and new social opportunities are just a few of the activities now within your grasp because contemporary seniors have opportunities their parents and grandparents never dreamed about.

—Uncover new facets of each other's personalities. Perhaps you've never known your husband other than as a working person. Now's the time to explore the dimensions of your mate's mind. There may be a man there you've never met, just as he may find there's a new woman in his wife—one who is just waiting to be discovered.

—Slow down your pace and set new priorities. Life with no deadlines, except for those you impose yourself,

is luxurious, and the opportunity to shed old responsibilities for more soul-satisfying pursuits is exhilarating.

Do not think of retirement as the beginning of the
end. Look forward to it as the beginning of what can
be the prime time of life for you and your husband.

The following keys outline a variety of real-life scenarios and offer solutions to problems that you and your
mate may encounter in retirement.

ACKNOWLEDGMENTS

There is no way I alone can take credit for this book. Acquaintances have trusted me with their problems and solutions, professional counselors and ministers have shared their time and expertise, and relatives have borne with me as I missed both meals and appointments.

Thanks to Bettye Gill and John Clyde of Oregon Retirement Planning Services in Salem, Oregon; Bruce Fairman, family counselor, Newport, Oregon; Donna Siegfried, family counselor in Oregon and Honolulu, Hawaii; Father Willis Steinberg of St. Paul's Episcopal Church and Pastor Ed Henderlite of First Congregational Church, Salem, Oregon; Dick Ackerman, who conducted retirement planning sessions in his position as head of the Human Relations Department of United Telephone Company of Iowa; Doug and JoAnne Raines of Globe Travel, Salem, Oregon; Jenee Orso, Automobile Club of Oregon; Katherine Fletcher, director of Oregon's Elderhostel program; Gay Abdon, director of programs at Salem Area Chamber of Commerce; Deb Craiger, director of Salem Senior Center, and George Bell and Ralph Wright, retired Oregon executives.

Special thanks to friend Sue Snook, who gave me the idea for a book on living with retired husbands; to Grace Freedson of Barron's, who appreciated my sense of humor; and to Judy Makover, my editor at Barron's, who kept my spirits up while calming me down.

And most of all, thanks to my husband of five years, Marv Goodman, for his help, love and support during this project. He's a world-class role model for a retired husband.

1

IS THIS THE MAN I MARRIED OR IS THERE A STRANGER IN HIS SHOES?

It's eight o'clock on a sunny morning and you're making the marital bed the same way you've made this bed every morning for 42 years. Suddenly you become aware of sharp eyes scrutinizing your every move.

"The sheets would be tighter and smoother if you finished off with a sharp right-angle military corner," comments a censorious voice from the doorway.

Who is this person telling you—a mother of five—how to make a bed?

This person is your mate, your beloved sweetheart and lover, the father of your children and the companion you promised to cherish for better or for worse.

So what is going on?

You, my friend, are living with a retired—spell that full-time—husband. A man who, up until a few weeks ago, had his own special niche in the workplace, a man whose days were structured and challenged by employment goals. His daylight hours had been filled with routines that made him a man among men. But now that is over.

Many personal counselors maintain that retirement is right up there with the most stressful situations a man can face—the others being birth, death, and puberty.

So what are you going to do with this retired husband who doesn't begin to resemble the employed husband you had before the banquet and the gold watch? Your

1

marriage has been, for the most part, a happy one and you want to keep it that way. You have both been looking forward to what the advertising world sentimentally dubs the "Golden Years." However, something has gone awry, and being the Earth Wife and Mother that you are, you want to fix it.

Whether you and your mate are long-termers in the marriage game or newlyweds, it's imperative that, to help her husband through this, a wife knows what goes on in her man's mind when he's been handed the tributes and shown the door. Sure, the dinner was great and the tributes were glowing, but do you really know what he was thinking that night? And all the days that have followed? It may be that your loved one feels that his life is over and he's useless—that (in his eyes) he's no longer a man.

The most important key to coping with a retired husband is to know that husband, says a personal counselor. Sure, you married the man, you sleep with him, and you may have borne him children. You know he turns squeamish if there's a vestige of yolk left uncooked in his morning egg. You also know he prefers his handkerchiefs ironed and still sheds a tear when Old Glory passes by. But do you really know this man?

It has been said that to a woman, love is everything, but that, to a man, self-proof is everything. Many a man finds his self-proof and sense of identity in the workplace, where there are constant goals to be met. Because of these demands he may develop a workplace personality entirely different from the one he displays at home. Men are rarely aware of this slow metamorphosis because they are not as likely as women are to spend time on introspection. Therefore, at the time of retirement, a man's work-self may be telling him that, because he is no longer part of the marketplace, he cannot possibly be the same person.

2

Take Walter and Chuck. For years, they had been supervisors in a Midwestern appliance factory which had a firm "30 years and you're out" retirement policy. Because they both had gone to work directly after graduation from college, their 30-year stints were up at 53. They were youngsters by today's "You're as old as you think you are" standards, but not by Walter's.

He'd put in his time, and now his work-self told him that his string was running out. What was left? The morning after his Friday night retirement banquet, Walter didn't get out of his bathrobe until nearly lunch. After lunch, he retired to the den and switched on the television. Soon his eyes drooped, and wife Millie heard snores emanating between sportscasters' commentary and cheery commercials.

"Is this my Walter?" Millie asked herself. Until now, Walter had been a weekend fireball, hurrying through chores so he'd be ready for the Monday morning wake-up call. "Well, this will pass," she told herself determinedly.

By the third week of retirement Millie was beside herself. After dragging himself from bed around 9:00 A.M., Walter rarely moved from the television.

Three blocks over, at Chuck's house, there was a radically different scenario. Chuck bounced up on the Saturday morning after his farewell dinner, grabbed his clubs, kissed wife Marilyn and disappeared to the golf course. Three months later, he was still deep into improving his game.

The difference between the two men is obvious. Walter lived for his work routine and it had disappeared, leaving him, he thought, without a lifeline. Chuck lived for his free time, and now there was plenty of time to spare.

While wife Millie was wringing her hands in worry, wife Marilyn was cheerily going about business as usual.

3

Some couples achieve midlife satisfaction with just a bit of fine tuning. Other relationships, as in the marriage of Walter and Millie, need major overhauls to survive.

But first, before getting to the step-by-step solving of this retirement survival plan, it is necessary for the reader to decide how much she is willing to give of herself and how much she should retain of herself to achieve an enriching and rewarding life for both herself and her mate. Key 2 will help you determine your role.

2

HIS RETIREMENT/YOUR PROBLEM: WHAT IS YOUR ROLE?

The first decision you must make as the wife of a newly retired husband is whether to stand back and let him work out his problems or plunge right in to help.

What is your role? Does the burden of his retirement happiness rest entirely on your shoulders? What does this man want from you during this period of adjustment? What exactly does he need? And, finally, how much are you prepared to give?

Certainly a wife should help ease her husband through a difficult period, but she should never do so to the extent of allowing herself to be bullied or to be used as a crutch. In a perfect world, a husband, should he find himself in a state of depression at the close of his work life, would practice some introspection, exercise self-discipline and take himself in hand to work out his problems.

However, as we all learned long ago, we do not live in a perfect world, and you may find yourself with a husband who is lost without his work and doesn't have a clue on how to find himself.

There are several emotions a woman may experience during the first few months of her husband's retirement.

A wife may feel:

Angry. The children are settled and are all functioning adults—at least, they were 30 minutes ago—

and although you miss them, you are not suffering from an empty-nest syndrome because you've rebuilt a nest designed for two. If you don't work outside the home, your life may be divided between home chores and meaningful activities you didn't have time for when you were a busy mother. These are your bonus years, and you were enjoying every moment until he retired and is now home to question your every move.

If you are employed, being able to come home to a peaceful environment after a busy workday has always been therapeutic because you and your husband, while he was working, had established an after-work routine designed to reduce your own personal stress levels. You're still slugging it out in the workplace, but now he is home waiting for you with emotional needs you may be too fatigued to fulfill.

Employed and at-home wives were interviewed, and reported that the resultant emotions range from frustrations to downright hostility.

Afraid. During the years, as a couple go busily about their day-to-day lives, they may not take the time to form deep friendships with each other. Suddenly, the "until death do you part" phrase of the wedding vow is a reality. When this moment of truth flashes, a woman may ask herself: "What's going to happen to us? I've been enough for him through our married life, but what if I'm not enough for him now? What if he is bored by me? What if I am bored by him? What if one is lacking for the other? What if . . .? What if . . .? What if . . .? There is nothing so terrifying as the fear of the unknown.

Trapped. The woman who feels trapped usually falls into one of two categories. She may be a wife who has spent her married life deferring to her husband, obeying the traditional male/female role plan outlined Lord knows how many years ago. What she wants has always come second, because to her way of thinking, the male, who has been her provider, should have the final say on all subjects of importance. Only since the children were grown and gone has she been able to enjoy the right of choice in her activities. And now that freedom is ending because he, that omnipotent HE who oversees her existence, will be at home 24 hours a day.

The second type of woman who feels that her mate's retirement may mean her entrapment could be a woman busy with a career she loves. She fears she will be trapped into making a choice between her husband and her career, and she wants them both.

If you feel any or all of these emotions, don't fret; they are perfectly normal. What you must do is learn how to deal with these worries.

In the transitional period just after retirement, the best plan is for a wife to back off. Don't crowd or smother your husband with suggestions, opinions and demands just now. Let him percolate a bit. Instead, focus on yourself and examine your own feelings about this transition and get your own self in order.

When you've done this, then you will be better able to discover exactly what the "inner man" of your man is experiencing and needing. This may not be an easy task because he may not know himself that well, but with love, understanding and perseverance, it certainly is not impossible.

Let's begin with the given. You do love this man, don't you? (If you don't, and think you want out of a miserable relationship, turn to Key 48 for some suggestions.) If you rate your love for your husband and your marriage as your number one priority, you must go about reviewing the extent of emotional damage, after the retirement ballyhoo has died down. Put your own fears on hold now because if you can help your mate ease successfully into his new lifestyle, then you may find that your own fears have been groundless.

3

IN TRANSITION: SUPPORTING THE INNER MAN

There may be another man in your life, one you have yet to meet, because the face your husband put on for the workplace may not have been the face he has presented to you, and because the face he has presented to you may not be the "inner face" of the man you married. Through either training or disposition, a man may not be able to, or even want to, share his most private self with anyone, even the woman with whom he has shared a life. If your mate has a predisposition toward inscrutability, uncovering the inner man may take some detective work, but it is imperative in order to help him achieve a successful retirement.

No matter how glowing the tributes were the night before, on the morning after his last working day the inner man must face three undeniable facts:

- That he has to stop being who and what he was. The work title is gone. The phone isn't going to ring with requests for an appointment or a meeting. There will be no employees or co-workers looking for decisions. There is no longer a secretary or an assistant to lend a hand or an ear. No co-workers to chat with. The work-self has simply ceased to be.
- That he is mortal and must take stock of his general health. Death can loom large to men of retirement age, and they invariably ask themselves, "How long have I got?" The aging process is a fearful threat.
- That he must acquire a new identity. If he is no longer

who he was, then who is he? He must don a new personality while retaining much of the old, and this may not be easy for a man of his years.

If these three facts terrify him, he may never share that with you, so don't be dismayed if he doesn't want to sit down and talk it all over.

"Men tend not to verbalize their feelings especially in areas of the unknown where they may be fearful," explains the director of a retirement planning service.

Keep a positive outlook, as it is very important that a wife be especially understanding and gentle during these first weeks.

Here are some tips from a facilitator for preretirement planning workshops on ways a wife can set the scene for her spouse to find meaning in his life:

- Easy does it. Don't force a nonstop schedule on him, but don't allow him time to sit and brood about the fact that life will never be the same. He might get to believing this, and then what will you have? A man who has no zest for life.
- Projects that need the expertise only he can provide or day trips to places you've never had time to visit are two gentle ways of easing him into this new life. Enlist the aid of your children if they're nearby. Most offspring will be delighted with a father who has time for both his children and their children.
- Be affectionately firm and supportive but not commanding when you're encouraging him to get involved in new hobbies and activities.
- You love this man, so put your personal interests and activities on the back burner for a while. The last thing a husband needs is a wife who is too busy to listen when he does speak. If he has an idea, accept it with enthusiasm, even if going to view spawning salmon at a nearby fish hatchery really isn't your cup of tea.
- Don't bombard him with questions about what he

10

wants to do. An interrogating woman, no matter how deftly she questions, can put a man on the defensive; and a man put on the defensive can go on the offensive in many ways.

• If you've gotten out of the habit of touching and showing affection, get back into that habit. He may wonder what's going on, but he'll never turn down a hug or a kiss. This is the time to reestablish the physical part of your relationship that may have been dormant during the last few years.

• Be willing to concede that you're not perfect—who is?—and that you may have to make concessions and perhaps change your wifestyle (see Key 10) to accommodate this radical restyling of your lifestyle.

Men tend to make friends with their co-workers. Retirement pulls them away from this support group. Help him work at forming new friendships with other men of all ages. If he does want to keep up with former co-workers, encourage him to meet them *after* work. A retiree who spends much time visiting at his former workplace can be a headache to those trying to work.

Sigmund Freud summed up the pain of retirement in *Civilization and Its Discontent,* written in 1929: "Work binds the individual more closely to reality and the human community."

Your husband is entering a transitional period that indeed may seem unreal to him. Make all the right wifely moves to cheer and support the inner man during this delicate period, and you're both going to reap the rewards in the years to come.

4

THE CASE FOR PLANNING YOUR RETIREMENT

"Couples often spend more time planning their summer vacations than they do their retirement," says the workshop facilitator of a retirement planning service. "Because of this casual approach to a serious time of life, retirement sometimes can be a frightening change of pace," she adds.

Although it is possible for some couples to pop into retirement cold turkey without too much trauma, some judicious planning with an expert can head off problems, because planning sessions give a couple some idea of what they should expect.

Facilitators take different approaches to seating arrangements in workshops, but the end result is often the same. In some sessions, spouses are at the same table, while in others they are separated to avoid one spouse dominating the discussion. But even when they are separated, they are generally placed at adjoining tables so that they can hear their mates' comments.

Whether side by side or at adjoining tables, the sessions are often eye-openers because spouses may discover facets of their mate's personalities, facets that had never surfaced during the busy years of building a career, making a home and raising families.

Take the case of Harve and Marian. Harve was a self-made man who had been a boss for so long he'd forgotten how to be an employee. A don't-rock-the-boat sort of wife, Marian's way of showing love was to give in to him on practically every turn of the way in their 40-year marriage. However, when it came time for him to hand over the company to a son, Marian did enroll herself and her hardheaded hubby in preretirement sessions.

Session seating is where the fireworks in the Harve and Marian saga began. Harve, sounding off in his usual way, was expounding at his table about *his* (got that?) retirement plans. He was going to move down to South Carolina and build a little cottage on the lot he'd already bought near the lake he'd fished at and enjoyed. He'd spend his time writing a book on how to found a successful company.

At the next table, Marian overheard this. "Pardon me?" was her reaction. "I'm hearing this for the first time. No, I don't intend to move out of the town where I've lived for 41 years. No, I do not want to live by that wonderful little lake. Don't you remember the mosquitoes? How the closest town with a hospital and proper shopping is 45 miles away?"

Harve was stunned. He was so used to making decisions for the family that it had never occurred to him to open up the communication lines with his wife and find out her ideas about retirement.

The resolution? They compromised—always the best way. Yes, they moved away from the northern winters and down to South Carolina, but no, they did not set up residence in a little cottage by a mosquito-infested lake. They bought a new condominium in a suburb of an old and charming city. Harve has easy access to the fishing he enjoys, and Marian has easy access to shopping, art galleries and various organizations.

Workshop facilitators say many wives blossom in these sessions. Women in the 60-plus age bracket generally were raised to play traditional roles in their marriages even if they worked outside the home and even if still employed, let their husbands make many of the marital decisions. "It is a pleasure to watch wives come alive and share feelings with their husbands, and amazing that it sometimes takes a public session to allow them the freedom," commented one facilitator.

Retirement planning programs tackle such topics as:

Opportunities. Retirement need not mean the end of a busy, fruitful life, when society is in dire need of older citizens with a variety of skills and expertise in many areas.

Where to live. The problems of whether to keep the big house or move to a smaller, more manageable dwelling and whether to relocate from a colder clime to a sunbelt area are discussed, with pros and cons explored in depth. Also talked about is the matter of security, often a problem with older couples who like to "lock it up and travel." Maybe a move to the security of a mobile home park or to a seniors-only complex would be desirable. If a move within the same city or area is contemplated, it may be wise to relocate before retirement so that your social and activity routines are already established.

Health and well-being. Good health practices do much to enhance the quality of retired couples' lives. Informative sessions with experts help them become aware of Medicare and supplemental policies and health services available to seniors, and offer simple "keep well" suggestions to carry out in their own lifestyles.

Legal affairs. Deciding whose name should be on the checking accounts and property, wills, probate and living trusts can be a puzzle to many who have not had legal training.

Income and budget planning. Many couples have taken their retirement income for granted and let financial plans slide. How best to make their money work for them is, however, of prime importance to couples who are retiring. "It is not what you make but how you spend which is the deciding factor in retirement," said a financial planning specialist.

Adjustment and activities. Psychologists help participants to understand what is happening to them and why they often feel as if their lives are over. Positive attitudes on retirement and retirement options such as second careers, part-time employment, challenging volunteer service or creative self-development are presented to couples who often haven't had time to check out their recreation options during a busy work life.

"Even the most savvy of couples often forget or neglect to discuss certain areas of retirement. Retirement planning courses are often eye-openers for seniors, and can help prevent some mind-boggling shocks," says one counselor.

For those in the preretirement age brackets who are interested in retirement planning, there are several possibilities. If you are working for a corporation, check with the personnel or human resources department about such a program. Your state's senior services agency may offer a planning program. Other sources might be the Community Service branch of your local community college, the YWCA, the YMCA or the Chamber of Commerce. If these organizations don't have a workshop schedule, they may include it in the future. And don't overlook your senior center or your local library for information on the subject.

5

THE FOUR C'S THAT MAKE RETIREMENT WORK

One of the greatest mistakes a woman can make is to assume that retirement is simply going to be a continuation of life as she and her husband have lived it for all their married life. Do not make this assumption! Life is not going to remain the same. When was it ever? Marriage is made up of the honeymoon period, the childbearing/child-raising years, the empty-nest years, and the retirement years. All are different, but the first three do have one common denominator: the husband and possibly also the wife have been out in the workplace. In retirement, whether one or both are retired, there will be major changes in the routines you two have established.

The fact that retirement years will be different from your previous years is no reason to panic. There are challenges to be met because the retired life requires a different approach to your lifestyle. Perhaps the most unsettling to a wife is that, unless you worked together in a business partnership, you and your husband are going to spend more time together than you ever have. Make that "MUCH MORE"—we're talking about 24 hours straight some days, unless he's retired and you're not.

Remember that old wives' saying, "I married him for better or worse, but not for lunchtime"? Well, it's time for lunch, and this can be a frightening realization unless a woman relearns and puts into practice the Four C's that are keys to making any relationship successful. The Four C's are communication, compassion, compatibility and compromise.

In the following keys, you will learn how to implement these C's into your day-to-day living, but first let me define them.

COMMUNICATION: Communication is a key factor in making any relationship work. Ideally, you and your spouse have been communicating since the day you met, but unfortunately this is not always so. Couples who communicated beautifully at the beginning of the marriage often have been so busy with jobs and children that communication has dwindled to the point that only the basic information gets put into words.

If you are living with a noncommunicator, your first step to opening up channels of communication is to define the type of spouse you have.

Do you have a husband who
1. Talks easily to men, but reluctantly to women, even his wife?
2. Rarely talks to anyone, even other men?
3. Talks constantly, but rarely says anything meaningful to a relationship?

Key 6 will discuss ways to deal with each of these problems of communication.

COMPASSION: To be able to experience and share the feelings of others is probably the most valuable of all human traits. Is compassion a learned trait or an innate ability? Certainly it is an attribute that many women possess, but, sadly, too many years of marriage may numb a woman's sensitivity where her husband is concerned. Witness the clubwoman who rushes out to serve meals to the needy and forgets to feed her needy husband at home. Sure, he could fix his own dinner and has done so on more than one occasion; but too often, longtime wives (and longtime husbands, as well) forget

17

that tender loving care can give the relationship the boost it needs to remain healthy for the years to come.

COMPATIBILITY: You've been trundling along like a pair of comfortable old shoes for nearly 50 years. Isn't that compatibility? Yes. Or maybe, no. Like most things, compatibility is relative and it has very little to do with having similar interests. Enriching your life by cultivating a loving and compatible relationship can be one of retirement's greatest rewards.

COMPROMISE: Mention this word to many women and the hackles rise. Why must it always be me who compromises? you may ask. With some insightful and creative thinking, the compromise can be made by both, but often it takes the wife to set the wheels of negotiation in motion.

So there are the Four C's: communication, compassion, compatibility and compromise. How are you going to put these ingredients, so vital to any relationship, back into your marriage? Let's begin with communication in Key 6.

6

COMMUNICATION: GET THOSE CHANNELS OPEN

Most wives realize that communication is what makes a relationship click, but it isn't easy to achieve if you're living with a man who won't or does not know how to communicate. If, however, you live with a man who communicates his feelings, wishes and thoughts openly and freely, count your blessings and move on to the next key.

But for many of us, how do you get a husband to open up and tell you what's on his mind when he's been relatively noncommunicative all his life? It's not the easiest task you've ever undertaken, but it's not impossible. You simply must make a game plan and follow through.

Make these your goals toward encouraging better communication:

- Seek information that will help you understand him and enhance your relationship. Nonthreatening questions and attentive listening will promote closer ties.
- Reveal your feelings so that he will understand you. Unless your mate is a mindreader, he won't know what you're thinking unless you tell him.
- Share information that is relevant to both of you, and get feedback on what he feels about the subject. If necessary, reflect or mirror back what he has said to you to be sure you've understood correctly.

Your game plan? Your first step might be to decide the kind of noncommunicator you're living with. In the previous key, we listed the three main types.

Type I: Doesn't really communicate well with women,

even you. One wife overheard her husband speaking to a male friend at a cocktail party.

"I was hearing things I'd never heard him speak of at home. I didn't realize that he had invested rather heavily in mutual funds and had lost several thousand dollars during the past 10 months. It was like a slap. He trusted a friend enough to unload this fact after several martinis at a party, but he'd never trusted me enough, his wife of 39 years, to tell me he'd had losses.

"On the way home, I told him, 'I feel very uncomfortable that you shared your mutual fund loss with Fred, but not with me. Can't we trust each other with our troubles as well as our triumphs?'

"He looked at me as if I'd lost my marbles and said, 'Of course I trust you. I didn't want to worry you.' "

In trying to protect Constance, Fred was shutting her out of his life while sharing with a male friend. He was appalled that she would think he didn't trust her.

Right then and there they agreed to ask and answer questions of each other on matters that count. Soon after, Fred began discussing stocks with Constance, and as a result she started giving him some suggestions. "I may not know much about the market, but I have hunches when it comes to some consumer stocks. We've made a little money and he respects my judgment," said a much happier Constance, who reported that, because of the after-party discussion, other communication channels are opening up.

Type 2: Doesn't say much of anything to anybody. Perhaps he comes from a family of nontalkers. Maybe his mother didn't say much and his father rarely talked at all. Possibly he had no siblings, further depriving him of the opportunity to communicate. When he does have something to say, he uses the fewest words possible. This can be wildly frustrating to a wife who likes to talk on practically any topic.

Ned and Doris were such a couple. Each Thursday night Ned took Doris out for Chinese food, and each Thursday, they ordered Family Dinner No. 3 and silently chomped their way through the almond chicken, fried rice, and sweet and sour pork.

One evening, Doris says, she couldn't take another mouthful. "I became queasy and there was a roaring in my ears. Well, I thought, here comes the heart attack that we women are warned about. I began talking to take my mind off what I thought of as imminent death. I blathered on about children who watched a lot of television being more hostile and aggressive than children who read or played games.

"Turned out Ned had been watching the same program in the den. Can you believe it? Two people in the same house, watching the same program in different rooms! We began discussing what we'd seen, just talking and talking as if we'd first met. I suddenly realized that I didn't feel sick any more. I was too busy talking to a husband I hadn't been really talking to for a long time. Isn't that silly? But isn't it wonderful that we could just begin to speak and to re-create a bond we haven't had for too many years?"

Doris spanned the communication gap by simply opening up her mouth and talking, something she'd pretty much given up on once the children began to arrive.

Her advice: Don't hold back. Speak out on what is interesting you at that particular moment. Talk about issues that are important to you and why. But don't just try to fill up empty air space. Make what you say interesting and phrase your thoughts into questions to ask what he thinks. It's also better not to ask questions that can be answered with a simple yes or no because that's what you may get.

Type 3: Never shuts up but doesn't really say anything

meaningful. This situation requires you to exercise compassion (see Key 7) and restraint, but let's try to figure out why he rattles on like this.

Men who talk too much without saying anything frequently suffer from the same fears as women who talk too much. They may lack self-confidence and self-esteem. They fear that what they say is not really important, but if they spout enough words enough times, people will begin to listen.

These inane chatterers often are constant tellers of jokes. Even the most loving of wives will occasionally contemplate physical force (murder perhaps?) to make them stop talking. Friends generally precede the wife's name by the word "long-suffering." A more serious variation of this type chatterer is one whose tales of business accomplishments or derring-do verge on pathological lies. Such a man is often regarded as a blowhard by friends and co-workers, and too often the couple's social life is nonexistent because of his actions.

The "too much talk/too little" problem may be solved by a simple discussion. Don't be accusatory as this may put your husband on the defensive. Simply say, "I feel uncomfortable when you . . .," and outline exactly why and when you feel uncomfortable.

Encouraging activities such as walking, hobbies and travel can promote conversational togetherness. Passive activities such as TV watching don't really encourage productive communication even though a mutually watched program did help open up the channels for Ned and Doris.

A simple and effective method to begin communicating is to say directly: "We need to talk. What would be a convenient time for you?" Your husband may be a bit wary, certainly curious, perhaps defensive, but set a time and stick to it and outline your needs.

When you sit down with him to share your feelings

or introduce a topic—personal or not—employ some follow-up questions such as:

—How or what do you feel about that?

—Tell me what you think.

—How does that strike you?

Then sit quietly until he answers. Many women—and I include myself in this category—do not wait for the husband's answer. We think that because an answer is not immediate, an answer is not coming, so we jump in to fill the silence. Remember, a dialogue is just as much listening as it is talking.

Perhaps you are married to a different type of communicator, one who doesn't verbalize much, but communicates by his actions that he is very tuned in to your needs and wants. Bless him, and learn to be bilingual, because *his* version of "husband-speak" lies in *demonstrating* how much he loves you. This man's actions speak louder than his words.

Before closing this section on communication, there's one more point to discuss: the disease one wife terms "husbandly selective deafness." Almost every marriage suffers from this disease occasionally, where a husband will simply tune out a wife if he's not particularly interested in the topic or if his mind is on other matters. For this reason, I strongly advise against instigating a "May we talk?" session during Monday Night Football or the NBA playoffs! However, if surrounding conditions are favorable, yet he continues to ignore your question or comment, try the "I feel hurt when I speak to you and you don't answer me" formula. If he replies, "I didn't think that statement [or question] needed an answer," assure him that it is important to you. If the behavior continues even after you've had the talk, do get him to a doctor specializing in hearing. Your spouse really may have a hearing problem.

You may never achieve the kind of communication

with your husband that you share with women friends, because women's friendships are based on sharing emotions and experiences while men's friendships are generally based on doing things together. But if you can define your husband's communicative behavior and set up a game plan and put it into action, you will get results.

Hopefully, once you two have begun to talk to each other, you'll be amazed at how much you do have to say to one another, no matter how many years you've been married.

7

COMPASSION: A GIFT FROM THE HEART

Compassion is a range of emotions, a gift from the heart that encompasses such qualities as understanding, sympathy, consideration, caring and forgiveness, but because we live in a "seize the moment" age of rush-rush and hurry-hurry, we too often overlook these simple and basic emotions when it comes to our mates.

As mothers, it is natural for us to feel deep and protective compassion for children as they flap their wings, sometimes with decided difficulty, on their way to independence, but as wives it is often easy for us to forget that our just-retired spouses are also flapping their wings, trying to fly in an environment that is totally alien to them.

This may sound overly dramatic, but while interviewing, I often heard women betray slight but unmistakable hardhearted and callous emotions about their floundering mates. Their behavior ranged from subtle verbal put-downs to downright cruelty, although had they been challenged on their actions they would have been amazed.

Clara was just such a woman. She and her husband, Gordon, had moved from the Midwest to be near their children—not always the smartest move. In the Midwest, Gordon had been a highly respected director of a bank, involved in a host of civic organizations and consulted whenever good judgment was needed for doings in their smallish city.

Once settled on the West Coast, Gordon was suddenly no one special—just another retired man in an adult-living community full of retired men. Never one to blow his own horn, Gordon didn't elaborate in public on his former accomplishments.

Neither did Clara, although there were many times she could have mentioned pridefully how respected her husband had been in their former home. Nor did she offer him respect and compassion in their home life. Ever so subtly, sometimes under the guise of humor, she began to put him down. New friends never got a chance to know the Gordon of his Prime Time, because all too soon, he began to dwindle in stature, self-esteem and physical health. Granted, his health problems may not have stemmed from his wife's lack of compassion, but they certainly weren't helped by it.

At the time of retirement, a man's life is irrevocably altered and his ego is fragile. A woman at ease in her environment and resentful of past grievances—perhaps real, perhaps imagined—can do a lot to make her husband's life hell on earth.

It is difficult to imagine why Clara chose to show such a cruel lack of compassion toward Gordon. Was she still carrying the emotional baggage of perhaps being a neglected wife of a busy executive? Was she getting even for a real or imagined sin he committed against her?

On the other hand, had she exercised warm compassion with a disoriented and perhaps frightened man, would his health problems not now be so severe? Maybe. But she certainly could have enriched the quality of his life.

Compassion may be a learned trait, and if so, the surest way to be a compassionate person is to have been born in a family whose members practice compassion for each other on a day-to-day basis.

Don't forget that compassion is a two-way street; if you feel that you are not getting enough in your rela-

26

tionship with your husband, don't be afraid to ask for it. Take newlyweds Billie and Mervyn, for example. Mervyn had an unfortunate habit of laughing at injuries. If Billie burned herself on the stove, he laughed and said, "That will teach you to put on an oven mitt." If she stumbled, fell, or dropped something, he laughed and said, "You never told me you were such a klutz."

One day, Billie had had enough. However, instead of lashing out, she said quietly, "Your lack of sympathy and compassion when I hurt myself is unkind and hurts me very much."

Mervyn was taken aback. "Well, that's the way my father always acted when Mom or I did something like that. He said if you laughed about something, it made it easier to bear," he blustered.

Not always. Since Mervyn, who truly loved Billie, learned that this type of behavior was upsetting, he has stopped laughing and does more hugging. The result? A happier marriage.

A tip for using compassion to ease retirement transition: Put the newfound channels of communication you learned in Key 6 into practice and try to discover your husband's biggest fears. Don't hesitate to tell him yours. When you make these discoveries, talk them out in a sincere and gentle manner. Never lapse into a recriminatory style of "If you wouldn't . . ." or "If you'd just . . ." and certainly never the destructive "You always . . ." Instead, use the most compassionate of phrases: "I love you. Let's put our minds and hearts to it and we'll get through this together."

Never ever view compassion as a display of weakness. Compassion is the essence of love.

8
COMPATIBILITY: KEY TO A COMFORTABLE RETIREMENT

The unhappiest couple I ever met were Mark and Lynn. They'd married out of desire mistaken as love and vowed before a minister and two hundred people that they would love and honor until death did them part.

The fact that they were in their late fifties at the time did nothing to dampen the ardor until the courtship and honeymoon were over and they were at home in their pricey condo. Then they discovered that they had absolutely nothing in common. In fact, they really grated on one another.

True, while in the courtship stage, Lynn had taken golf lessons so she could play golf with Mark. True, she had taken skiing lessons so she could ski with Mark. True, she had taken tennis lessons so she could play tennis with Mark. So they had golf, they had skiing, they had tennis as common interests, and their love-making was terrific, but it didn't take them long to realize that a couple must get off the course, the slopes, the court and the sheets some time or other. There is that inescapable matter of day-to-day living.

And that's when Mark realized that life with his first wife, Margaret, hadn't been particularly exciting, but it sure had been comfortable.

The happiest couple I ever knew were Frank and Rose. He fished. She didn't. He golfed. She didn't. He played gin rummy. She didn't. Their sex life was not explosive, but warm and comfy. They were married at the same age as Mark and Lynn, but there was one extra ingredient in their marriage: Frank and Rose were compatible.

Simply defined, compatibility is the marvelous mix of mutual respect for your mate's needs and a tolerance for each other's foibles plus being accepted and loved for the person you are. Or as one psychosocial counselor put it: "Compatibility is not so much doing things together as it is feeling safe enough to do things separately."

Lynn had completely remade herself to accommodate Mark. She even took Cordon Bleu cooking lessons so she could impress his friends. Rose, on the other hand, cooked a heck of a good meatloaf. Rose waved goodbye to Frank as he went off to golf or fish with his buddies, and she was there when he got home, happily reading a book or watching her favorite TV programs. And there was always a warm kiss and supper in the oven, and if their lovemaking didn't move the earth, it satisfied them very much.

At no time in a marriage will compatibility be more important than at the time of retirement. A couple who, during working years, spent no more than 40 percent of their time together may have been compatible, but in retirement they may spend 70 to 90 percent of their time in union. This togetherness, so cherished by honeymooners, can wear thin when you're up in your sixties and retired.

Using compassion and communication, you and your husband should sit down and discuss how you both can be comfortable in retirement, because it is the responsibility of each partner to tell the other what makes him or her comfortable.

Here are some possible problem areas:

- Routines. He used to leave early for work. You lounged around with a cup of tea watching the "Good Morning, America" show before you launched into housecleaning. Now there may be a man looking to you for breakfast and companionship.
- Television. This may sound trivial, but it was a complaint voiced by several wives. "There is one television, and he controls it. I am far more willing to listen to programs he chooses than he is to listen to mine."
- Temperature. Don't laugh—the temperature of your house can create a pitched battle if one of you gets the chills at 68 degrees while the other has heat prostration at anything warmer. I read somewhere about the woman who calls herself the "Little Sister of Perpetual Cardigan" because she has to wear a sweater in her own kitchen, hubby being a tough taskmaster for cutting the heating bill!
- Telephone calls. You're not going to believe how interested he will be in your telephone calls. "Who was that?" "What did they want?" Most aggravating is the remark, "You'd get a lot more work done if you didn't talk so much on the phone!"
- Comings and goings. "Where are you going? What time will you be home?" What is this? Doesn't he trust you?
- Division of labor. He expects you to perform the same chores you did before he retired, even though you're still working full-time.

If the prospect of these mostly minor problems is dismaying, here are some tips for making your life together more comfortably compatible:

- Routines. If he's going to be home all the time, there's no reason for you to hop to fix his breakfast unless you want to. It's your retirement, too, and remind him of that—but do it lovingly and keep your sense

30

of humor. Don't get angry; just get your cup and settle down for your favorite program. Don't let yourself be bullied. A little time to get set for the day never hurt anyone. Happily, most men do learn to fix their own coffee, and very often wander in to watch TV with their wives. Great! Morning talk shows can provide conversational fodder for a good part of the day.

- Television. Television is prime entertainment for retired couples. Is there anything more irritating than a man with a remote control in his hand clicking your life and your favorite programs away in the search for a ball game? Save your household money and buy a second TV. Put it in the bedroom or the den if one is not already there. Announce that one of the TVs is at your disposal—no fair his trying to watch two different ball games on two TVs, as did one rascally husband.

- Temperature. One woman I know (me) proved her point by getting bronchitis on a regular basis. I didn't plan it that way and certainly didn't enjoy the illness, but it did teach my loved one that I am a hothouse flower when it comes to a chilly home. However, I changed my ways by compromising on the temperature about two degrees, cuddling under a fuzzy blanket while I watch TV, and remembering to turn off the lights when I leave the room. That's my way to keep utility bills down and my husband happy.

- Telephone calls. Keep down the length of your calls. Sure you can do it, even when you're talking to your best friend. Try to use the telephone when your husband is out on an errand. After a call, when interrogation begins, hold onto your sense of humor as you report the who, what, why and when. If it makes him happy, why hide the information?

- Comings and goings. Stay calm. Of course he trusts you; he just misses you. And it isn't the end of the world to have someone interested in your departures and returns—think of the lonely alternative. Verbally check in. You're not a teenager reporting to a parent again, but a loving wife telling a husband where you're going and when you're coming home—but make the time approximate lest he be waiting with a stopwatch.

• Division of labor. You're working at your job and at your home, too? Time to sit down and tell him exactly how you feel about this unfair division of labor now that he's home all day and you're still employed outside the home. Key 28 will help you outline possible solutions.

Compatibility after retirement? It's relatively easy to achieve if you both keep your sense of humor and your perspective; if you respect each other's wishes, space, and privacy; and if you both are willing to talk things over and make adjustments.

9

COMPROMISE: JUST ANOTHER WORD FOR NEGOTIATION

Say "compromise" to some women and watch them bristle. I don't know why. Compromise is not a negative collapse of principles. It is a positive approach to solving a mutual problem; and nowhere is compromise more important than between a man and a woman who want their marriage to work.

In the previous key on compatibility, compromises were discussed on such minor irritations as telephone calls, temperature, television habits and routines, but in this key compromise takes on more serious connotations.

Dave and Teresa bucked heads after they both retired. They had been born in a small town and had lived all their married life there. Teresa, happy with family and friends around her, saw no reason to change their situation. Dave confessed that he yearned for full-time life at their coastal condominium.

They leased their home to their daughter and took off for the coast. Once there, Dave became a happy and contented wharf rat, working on his fishing boat and talking with other sailors at the marina.

Teresa was not so happy, but she was smart enough to count her assets. Her husband, who had worked physically hard all his adult life, was delighted with their new lifestyle. They both had their health. Living in a lovely condo with a beautiful view was not exactly the epitome of suffering, she reasoned. "But I miss my children and grandchildren and my friends. What can I do about this?" she thought.

She waited until one evening after supper and then spoke to her husband. "I love you very much, but I miss our children and my family. Although I have given in to your wishes to live here, I am not entirely happy. I have a compromise in mind. How about it?"

What Teresa had in mind was alien to his idea of marriage, but he listened. She wanted to drive home—alone or with him, whichever he pleased—and visit family for several days every other week. The visit was to last no longer than three days. If Dave chose not to come, he'd have to cook, do household chores and be alone. Could he handle it?

Dave was amazed that she had been unhappy. Since she had gone along with his retirement wishes, he thought she was looking forward to this new life as much as he was. Now, realizing that she was lonely, he quickly agreed; he was as sincerely eager to please his wife as she was to please him.

The compromise worked. Sometimes he drives home with her, sometimes not. But taking care of their condo home, he now has even more respect for Teresa, remembering how she managed three children and a large house while working eight hours a day. Teresa, happy with the knowledge that she can go "home" whenever she chooses, has relaxed and begun to ease into the life of her new community.

If problems do develop and you feel a change of some kind is in order, here are some tips on how to artfully negotiate a compromise:
• Sit down with your mate and outline the problem as you see it. Sometimes the situation will resolve itself; perhaps your mate didn't even realize that you were unhappy.
• Don't begin the discussion on a negative note with

34

weepy or hostile recriminations. Explain your feelings calmly and rationally.

- Once you've stated your case, end your part of the discussion with a question such as "How do you feel about this?" or "What are your thoughts?"
- Don't let yourself be shouted down by an angry man. If his voice begins to escalate, sit quietly. Never shout back; you'll get absolutely nowhere. When he slows down and you realize that there will be no give-and-take at this parley, tell him quietly: "I'm sorry you're upset. Why don't we pick up this subject when you're in a better mood?" Don't placate him or assume complicity with his lack of control or reason. Your calm manner will tell him that you don't intend the subject to be dropped.
- If he begins to state his side of the issue, sit back and listen. Do not interrupt him. You are in a dialogue, and that means you're probably on your way to a compromise.

10

A NEW WIFESTYLE CAN MEAN A NEW LIFESTYLE

What is a wifestyle? Do all married women have one? And if we do, why would we want to change?

First: A wifestyle is the manner in which you deal—and I don't mean this disparagingly—with your husband. Clever women create and maintain positive wifestyles that will keep their men interested for years. Others have developed negative styles such as nagging, whining and bullying. Yes, women can bully men very successfully, but who really wants to?

Second: Do all married women have a wifestyle? Certainly, whether you realize it or not. Some wives have positive styles that make their husbands feel comfortable, contented and coddled, while others have unproductive styles that numb any spontaneity from their husbands.

Examples of wifestyles? Here are two, Lucille and Lynette. Lucille, an abrasive type, never softened her style when it came to communicating with Les, a gentlemanly and intelligent bookkeeper. Lynette, a quiet woman, was ever gentle when speaking to her husband, Dick.

Third: Why should a woman want to change her style? Let's allow the two wifestyles to speak for themselves.

"Why play games? I was who I was then and I am the same now. We've been married 44 years. Why should I change?" says Lucille, who bossily bulldozes her way through life.

In a restaurant, she cuttingly reminds her husband that if he eats onions he knows very well he's going to spend the night being miserable. She may be sincerely concerned about his health, but she's so brusque, he cringes at the sound of her voice.

Why not be a sorceress like Lynette? Unlike Lucille, Lynette softcoats her admonitions to Dick.

"Sweetheart," she'll say, leaning toward him at the dinner table and softly touching his arm, "I know you love those onions, but you may not feel well later."

These women may come across as one-dimensional stereotypes, but they are very real women, so I've used their radically different wifestyles to illustrate.

There are many styles. Perhaps you're the passive wife. Do you wearily accept your life because you don't have the energy and imagination to make it better? Are you the woman who realizes that married life should be more than a grudging coexistence but who is afraid that a suggestion for change might mean a confrontation? I hope you're not an indifferent wife—one of the worst wifestyles. An indifferent wife is one who is so into herself or so insensate that she neither cares nor worries what is happening to her husband.

Gen was a mix of three styles. She was passively reluctant to change, but she did realize that married life should offer more than what she had with Len. And there was a tad of indifference in Gen's makeup because she had neglected to tune in to her husband.

Married just after World War II, Leonard became a CPA while Gen worked in an office until the children began to arrive. After the children were grown, Gen didn't return to work. She decided she was too far out of touch with her secretarial skills, so she devoted herself to a constant round of volunteering, always making it a point to be home when Leonard arrived home for dinner. After dinner, she sat on *her* sofa and read or did handwork, Leonard sat in *his* recliner, TV clicker in his hand. Rarely did they go out, except for church or a visit to the children.

If you'd asked whether she was happy, she might have said, "I'm not unhappy."

When time came for retirement, Leonard was given a send-off banquet which included the firm's entire staff. This was Gen's first look at Leonard's office life *in toto*. She was stunned. Leonard—his co-workers called him Lennie—was the star of the show. From the lowest clerk, a panther-slim blonde in a Spandex miniskirt, to the firm's head bookkeeper, Lennie was everyone's chum.

The Leonard she lived with was an antisocial man while his workself was a social animal. Lennie was so wrapped up in his workplace that he was getting all the social strokes he needed at work. It was not that Leonard didn't love Gen or didn't want to be an involved spouse, but since he'd already had his social life at work, home was just a place to rest up until the next day. Their retirement years were in grave danger of being an unhappy and sterile period until death did them part.

Gen got angry, so angry she began to make some changes in her life, and although she didn't realize it, she was about to make some radical changes in her wifestyle.

The first thing she did was to rearrange her volunteer schedule at the hospital, going from daytime back-office work to night duties at the reception desk. Let him learn his way around the kitchen, she thought. Now in the public eye, it wasn't long until she took a good look at her appearance and realized that she was neat and clean but frumpy. A co-worker recommended a good salon, and within days Gen had a new hairstyle, her graying hair highlighted with blonde streaks. She updated her wardrobe, and enrolled in a beginners' bridge class on a free night.

On the other hand, Leonard, deprived of his daily social life, began to wilt. Gen noticed, to her horror, that Leonard was not shaving every day and he was becoming sloppy in dress and appearance. Her righteous "get out and get even" attitude dwindled as compassion set in. She remembered the man she'd fallen in love with, the man who had been a good father, and a kind and gentle provider. What could she do to help him?

She put her imagination to work. Checking with the curriculum adviser at the community college, she learned that the college was in dire need of an instructor to help senior citizens with their taxes. A word to the adviser, delighted with a live expert who didn't need much pay, elicited a letter to Leonard asking if he'd teach a few courses.

The result? Her recharged husband began to revive, but this wife wasn't about to let the classes become his only social life. Clever Gen complained one morning that her bridge class needed one more member. Would Leonard—whom she'd begun calling Lennie, incidentally—sit in?

Maybe just once, he said. Once was enough; bridge appealed to Leonard's neat, logistical brain, and he was hooked. Now the two laugh, talk and play together. They have become bridge masters and attend statewide tournaments, and have been asked to head a bridge tournament on a cruise.

Does this smack of manipulation? Not really. Gen just changed her wifestyle from passive to aggressive because she wanted something more with her husband in retirement.

In any relationship, partners are equally responsible for making the relationship work, but it certainly doesn't hurt to take a good long look at yourself. There may be things you could be doing to spark things up on the home front. Here are some suggestions:

- Be brutally honest with yourself. Are you boring? How will you know? Make a list of topics you discuss with your husband on a daily basis. Do the same topics turn up day after day? You're boring him, and he's probably boring you. Back to the communications key again. Read, listen and learn so you will be informed on what's going on in your community, your state, your nation and the world. Then make a point of bringing up at least one and hopefully more new topics each day.

- Have you become a trifle sour and cynical about the way your life and marriage have turned out? Is life simply a routine of putting one foot in front of the other and getting through the day? One counselor maintains that the only difference between a rut and a grave is the size of the hole. Get out of that negative rut and into some positively different interests that will get him involved, too.

- Are your friends the same ones you've had for ages? And they're all couples? Add new friends to your social list. Organizations, classes, church, volunteer groups offer wonderful ways to meet new people. Senior organizations provide a world of entertainment, but don't limit your new acquaintances to those your own age.

- Are you one of the selfish wives? When was the last time you put his welfare above your own? Make a record of how many hours you spend pleasing yourself and how many hours you spend pleasing him. Don't go overboard on organizational activities, like Hallie. She had a wonderful job and was an avid community worker. She was so caught up with being on this board and that board that she neglected her husband,

Arland. It took a near breakup to realize how far she'd drifted from being the loving wife he'd married seven years before. After some counseling, she learned how to prioritize and organize her home, work and club time.

- When was the last time you made him laugh? Do you even know what tickles his funny bone? When was the last time *you* laughed? Do it more. Laughter is infectious.
- Made a pass at him lately? Of course not, you say. You've been married too long for that. Ridiculous! If he's around after you read this sentence, give him a hug and a kiss, and tell him that you love him.
- Do you whine? Are conversations with your husband loaded with complaints? The answer to this is ridiculously simple—although most of us ignore the obvious solution—think before you speak. I once reflected on a conversation I had with my husband, and counted six complaints I'd made, some with heavy-handed humor, within a ten-minute period! Just as bad, when things aren't going your way, do you adopt a martyred saint attitude? Don't righteously sulk. Voice your dissatisfaction quietly and rationally. Let your husband know what's on your mind.

Statistics aren't in or even recordable, but I guarantee you that most husbands will respond to a tender, laughing, imaginative wife who practices a positive wifestyle.

11

DEFINING YOUR RELATIONSHIP

Yesterday's retired couples are not always the retired couples of today. Although many retirement-age couples are celebrating their 40-plus wedding anniversaries, many others are not. Contemporary couples have a wide variety of lives and lifestyles.

Defining the makeup of your marriage and the type of couple you two are can be the first step toward creating a comfortable stress-free retirement, because each lifestyle needs a different wifestyle to handle the situation.

Here are examples of some typical couples of today:

RAY AND KARLENE: They met while in high school. Ray went into the service, returned and married Karlene, who worked to allow him to attend college on the GI bill. A dedicated worker, Ray rose in his company, and Karlene kept on working as a legal secretary. Their lives were geared around their work and their family. They did have a few friends of their youth, but there was never enough time to get out and make new friends, because they were too busy with work during the week and with home and family during the weekends. Karlene had a few women friends among her co-workers, but she had never joined any organizations.

When the children left home and married, Karlene continued to work part-time, but after the grandchildren began to arrive, she volunteered to quit and act as baby-sitter. They provided company because Ray was now traveling for his company. Karlene refused to travel with him, saying that "the grandchildren" needed a strong home base while their parents worked.

After Ray retired and their son and daughter-in-law moved with their family to another city, Ray and Karlene, nearly strangers by now, looked at one another and wondered, "What do we do now?"

Their plight is typical of many couples. They had not grown together. Because of the nature of his business, Ray was light-years ahead of his wife in terms of intellect, sophistication and worldliness. Because she realizes she hadn't kept up, Karlene is fearful of new experiences outside the narrow sphere she had created for herself.

DONALD AND DIANA: There are a lot of Donalds and Dianas in today's world. They were both young when they married other partners. Neither marriage took, and both were divorced. They met when Donald was 58 and Diana was 48. He was a state attorney; she had worked up to be office manager at a medical clinic.

These two led happy and productive lives until Donald retired at 65, a forced retirement because of state policy. Diana, 55, was at the peak of her career, making good money and enjoying every moment of her challenging job.

Nearly overnight, their life changed. Diana had no intention of quitting her position, but Donald had become a demanding and grouchy husband. Now she is at her wit's end trying to keep up with the demands of her job, yet ensure that her at-loose-ends husband is happy and busy.

FRAN AND WILBUR: When asked about their friends, Fran would chirp: "We don't need friends. We have our children."

Many of their contemporaries complained that their children were scattered about, and that, consequently, they were not getting to know their grandchildren. Fran and Wilbur's solution was to sell their home, buy a recreational vehicle and traverse the country, visiting each of their five children in turn. They'd roar up in their RV, perfectly sure of their welcome, and usually end up moving into their children's spare bedroom.

To "earn their keep," Fran and Wilbur helped out around the house. She took over the cooking, and he began fixing everything he could find that needed fixing. These two were divinely happy. They were, they'd tell themselves proudly, a real part of the lives of their children and grandchildren. They hadn't spotted the fact that their welcome was wearing thin until one day Fran overheard her daughter-in-law say: "Get that woman out of my house. I don't care if she is your mother. She's driving me crazy."

Fran and Wilbur were crushed. They'd tried to live their lives through their children, only to find out that their children didn't want that much family participation. The couple, with energy to spare and in love with their nomadic existence, are now faced with the prospect of taking a good hard look at a retirement that wasn't working out as they had planned.

NORB AND JUANELLE: There was an instant attraction between these two, who met at a tavern frequented by employees at a nearby newspaper. The couple were thrown together one night by simple proximity of side-by-side seating. By the next week they were inseparable and began planning a retirement togetherness.

Norb, in the midst of a divorce, had eight more months before retirement at 62. Widowed at 55, Juanelle, now 57, decided that life with Norb was far more interesting than working on the inserter at the newspaper.

They, were married the day after Norb's divorce

became final, and began to make plans to travel about the country, seeing all the sights they'd missed during a hardworking life.

Unfortunately, life is not always fair. Several weeks after their retirement, Norb collapsed with a stroke and their happy plans were put on hold. Juanelle finds herself at home with a terrified and angry husband who is afraid his life is over.

SAM AND SHERRIE: Sam, a dynamic corporation director, and Sherrie are another just-married couple. Sherrie, a young (32) but wise-in-the-ways-of-men secretary in Sam's company, had successfully waged an assault upon the senses of this older man, who was soon reeling under the attention of the slender redhead.

It didn't take Sherrie long to become a part of Sam's life. Why not? She was the cheerleader he'd never had in high school.

Although Sam, 65, may seem to be besotted with his much younger wife, she has found that he's really a tough customer to live with. She knows that his mouth can be mean and that he's not above physical cruelty when he's been drinking, but when he was so busy working, it really didn't matter. She could take the abuse while enjoying the country-club life of credit cards, travel and leisure.

Then Sam retired, and now Sherrie is trapped with a crotchety man who feels his prime is past and who is suspicious of the lifestyle of his young wife.

BOB AND BONNIE: These two met in first grade. By the time they were in junior high, they had decided they were in love, and they were married just after high school graduation.

"I don't remember a time when Bob wasn't right there," said Bonnie, who took a secretarial course while Bob attended college. "When he graduated and opened an insurance business, it seemed natural that I would slip right in as secretary. We've spent every working day together for the past 46 years."

Is there such a thing as too much togetherness? Because they were so close in age, they even retired together, and now they're at home—still together and wondering what to do with the empty hours.

Although there are variations of these six couple-scenarios these are the most typical of contemporary couples of retirement age. The next keys will deal with each couple in turn, listing ways they can put new life into their new lifestyles.

12

DON'T LET A GROWTH GAP SPOIL YOUR RETIREMENT

While in Japan two years ago, I spoke with a young professor about the divorce rates in his country. It was an eye-opener to discover that many older Japanese couples are divorcing because they virtually do not know each other and have nothing in common. Their marriages had been arranged by parents; the husband worked long hours; the wife stayed home with the children. When he came home to stay after retirement, they looked upon each other as strangers.

Although American marriages are rarely arranged, there are similar situations among our retired couples. In a long-term relationship, one person may outdistance the other in terms of intellect, sophistication, and ability to function in more worldly ways. The result is that, when time for retirement arrives, you painfully discover that you and your spouse have few things in common, and the reason you tolerated each other in a marriage rut is that you have spent the majority of the time apart.

This was the problem faced by Ray and Karlene in Key 11. While Ray grew as a person through work opportunities such as personal growth and management seminars and business-related travel, Karlene refused to venture into the outside world via organizations, travel with Ray, classes (either work or nonwork related), study groups or even books. Her days were as predictable as the route of a carousel horse.

The problem in reverse was the marriage of Nina and

47

Ed. Struggling to keep a small business afloat, Ed had gotten himself into a workaholic rut. After raising three children, Nina went to work at a newspaper, first as a proofreader, then as a reporter. Her job was challenging and exposed her to a great variety of people, ideas and lifestyles. Gradually, Ed withdrew even more to his workplace and Nina to hers. By the age of retirement, there was no chance of this marriage making it because she was part of the world outside work, while he was virtually a prisoner in his work.

"I wish we'd talked more about what was happening to us," said Nina.

If your marriage is on the verge of disaster because you've grown apart, you two have some major adjustments now that he's retired and back home. If you haven't attended a retirement planning seminar, it will be tougher, but take heart. There are ways to kick-start a sluggish marriage and get it back on line before it is too late, as it was with Nina and Ed.

No matter whether you're the wife who has been left behind or the wife who has forged ahead, it may be up to you to begin to bridge the growth gap. Over a cup of coffee, a glass of lemonade or sips of a dry martini—whatever's your pleasure—it's time to say: "I know we've grown apart, but what are we going to do about it? Let me hear what you think."

If he looks restlessly from side to side, begins to finger the television remote control nervously, then says, "I think I wish you'd fix supper and let me listen to the Lakers," you may have picked the wrong time to ask the right questions. If so, kiss him and go to prepare dinner, but tell him you're going to ask the same question again when the ball game is over.

If he appears receptive but still silent, begin to describe your own feelings and how the apartness is affecting you and how you feel about your marriage. If he remains silent, tell him you'd like to hear him describe his feelings on the subject.

After he answers, ask him these three questions:

—If we could do anything we want today, what would you want it to be?

—If we could do anything we want for a week, what would you want it to be?

—If we could do anything we want for the rest of our lives, what do you think we should do?

These questions sound sophomorically simple, but the answers are important because the word "we" figures so prominently. Listen to what he says. This is the here and now of retirement, and it's important for you to get him to talk so you can listen closely to his answers and discover what's making him tick.

Breaking away from the preretirement routine, whether it be the problem of having grown apart or of removing yourselves from a mind-paralyzing rut, may be easier than you think, because today there are so many activities a couple can enjoy on any income.

Here are some hints to get your relationship and your marriage back into the mainstream:

• Be agreeable if he's off and running to a new activity that is contrary to your own idea of a good time. A boat show, perhaps? Ask to go along. Don't be afraid to try something new. The next turn will be yours. Be prepared with something crazily different. How long has it been since you two took in a 2:00 P.M. matinee at the movies complete with big bags of popcorn?

• Seek out new interests, such as joining an organization together. If you have a shy man, try to make sure the organization is one in which he'll feel comfortable. It may take attending several organizations to find one

you're both comfortable with. If you're the shy one, grit your teeth and go forth with a positive attitude. You may like it, and your marriage will prosper.
• Try to do one new thing together each week, whether it's attending a concert in the park or the opening of a fancy new supermarket.

Whatever you do, you're getting out of the rut and into a new experience. And the most important part: You're doing it together and you're beginning to bridge the gap.

13

HE'S RETIRED/SHE'S NOT

When Donald retired at 65, Diana was 55 and at the peak of her career. She had worked her way up from file clerk to supervisor in a large state agency.

Donald and Diana are typical of today's older working couples, and their "he's retired/she's not" situation is becoming more common as more woman moved out into the workplace. Department of Labor statistics report that in the 55–59 age group 52.2 percent of women are working and in the 60–64 age group 33.2 percent are employed.

As this statistic points out, the majority of women under 60 are still in the work force; therefore, most of their husbands are in the retirement age bracket (55 and older). Although the usual retirement age is 65, Department of Labor statistics report that 33 percent of American men aged 55–64 are now out of the work force, up from 28 percent in 1980. Some men have been forced into early retirement, posing an especially delicate problem, since being forced into retirement when you're not expecting it can be devastating.

When a man has retired and his wife is still working, a host of problems may arise. For many of these couples, theirs is a second marriage. They met and fell in love while both were vital and involved people. Now that's changed, and because of reversal of roles, their marriage is not without perils when it comes to peace and contentment on the home front.

Donald knew Diana was a gregarious and strong woman, because these were the qualities that had attracted him. He was a power in state government, and his dominant personality and presence had been like a magnet to a younger Diana, just trying her social wings when the two met and fell in love at a political party.

Now his work life has ended and hers is at its zenith. They love each other very much, but both admit that keeping that love alive was a struggle when Donald first retired.

How did she handle the situation?

DIANA: "There was a tremendous period of adjustment. Suddenly I was on the inside and there he was on the outside looking into a world where he'd been a power broker. For many months he was aimless—spent a lot of time on the couch watching CNN and reading books. His lack of initiative regarding routine or activities frightened me, and I reacted by nagging, I'm sorry to say.

"Gradually, I realized that this was no way to proceed. I needed to set my priorities. I realized that my husband and our marriage were my number one priority at this moment, because he was at the most vulnerable period of his life. He certainly didn't need a wife grousing about him being unproductive. I knew he wasn't lazy. He just didn't know how to proceed from this point. If he was going to get involved again it was up to me.

"We had always been interested in politics, and a friend was running for state assembly. I had the friend call Donald and ask for our help. When I got home that evening, he reported that we were needed. I immediately agreed. He was off the couch and back into the mainstream. From his work on the campaign, Donald then was asked to be on a state and a city board.

"Also, once he was off the couch, he noticed how much weight he'd gained, and he began walking and working out at a gym to take off the extra pounds. Now he is as busy and involved as I am."

Diana and other working women interviewed offer these tips for career women with retired husbands:

- Realize that there is going to be a period of transition after retirement and that he is going to need your help. Be willing to put your career on the back burner. "Don't push, don't nag, as I did," said Diana. "It doesn't help. Give him some time to find himself."
- When you come home and find he's sulky or grumpy, keep out of his way. Go about your home business quietly and act as if nothing is wrong. A hovering wife doesn't make him feel any better. Quiet support he needs, pity he doesn't.
- Really hear what he has to say. Take the time to listen and give him lots of positive feedback on his opinions and suggestions. When he's done a chore or gotten out in the community, give him strokes. Again, remember how vulnerable this man is.
- Share your life with him. You'll be surprised how much more interested he is in your work now that he's not worn out from his own. One tip from a woman who found out the hard way what not to do: When sharing work experiences, don't constantly mention male co-workers. If the subject comes up naturally, so be it, but don't go overboard on stories involving how you and Clyde had so much fun solving your office problems. Any husband, retired or not, can feel threatened when other men's names constantly roll off his wife's lips.
- Establish special routines that you both look forward to. One wife reports that Friday night was their evening to unwind before he retired, and she saw no reason the fun should end. Her husband still meets her in their favorite watering spot, where politico types gather after work. They have a drink and go on to dinner at new and different places.
- Keep up with the friends you had before his retire-

ment. Don't let him withdraw from the company of working men. One wife said: "There was a period when I couldn't get him to mingle with friends we'd had for years. One night, he said, 'What do I have to contribute anymore?' I answered, 'Forty years of experience and a mind that still works very well.' "

- Don't expect him to change his ways just because he's home all day. If he didn't like to do housework before he retired, don't think a miraculous transformation is forthcoming. If he wasn't a cook before he retired, don't expect gourmet meals awaiting you.

- If there are chores you'd like him to attend to while you're at work, make suggestions, but don't leave orders. Men may laugh about stridently directive "Honey, do" lists, but their laughter is hollow.

- For many men, sex is the proof that they are still alive and vital. Don't be surprised if your at-home husband suddenly wants to make love quite often, sometimes before you've even slipped out of your work clothes.

Diana advises working wives to have patience with their recently retired husbands. If your marriage is healthy to begin with, the retirement stage will turn out just fine. The old routines will be supplanted with new routines that will become just as comfortable in time. Just remember to love him, love him, love him and make him feel you need him more than ever.

14

"IN SICKNESS AND IN HEALTH . . ."

Remember Norb and Juanelle, the unfortunate new-lyweds whose retirement hadn't turned out as they had anticipated? They'd met and married in a fever and planned a happy retirement on the open road in a new RV. Then Norb suffered a stroke just a few weeks after they both retired.

The older we get, the more we discover that life is not always fair, and Norb and Juanelle are prime examples of such inequity. After years in unhappy marriages, they had found each other and planned a new life only to have it snatched away by an unkind fate. Unfortunately, theirs is not an uncommon story. A couple retires, and shortly thereafter one falls ill, leaving the other partner to be both mate and caretaker.

We'll not dwell on the whys of these misfortunes, although some counselors see a correlation between men stopping work and their falling ill. These counselors say that it is not uncommon for a man to be so wrapped up in his work, he simply ceases to exist without it and quickly becomes ill, or even dies. This was not Norb's case. The blustery truck driver was eager to get away from daily newspaper deliveries and begin piloting a vehicle on the highways of life, his new partner at his side.

What happens to the spouse—and it is most often the wife—who has entered into retirement only to find that the title of nurse has been added to her duties?

"You cry a lot," said Juanelle, who felt cheated of the happiness she'd had so little of. "Yes, you do cry a lot," confirmed Mae, who had been married 46 years to a man who was diagnosed with a debilitating disease shortly after retirement.

So there is no difference. Six months or 46 years, you're going to feel hurt, cheated and baffled by what has happened to you.

In Juanelle's case, Norb, always an active type, became angry and temperamental after the stroke left him with a partially paralyzed left side and a loss of speech. Not only was Juanelle deprived of a new life, she was married to a man whose temper tantrums grew nearly unbearable.

Mae's situation was different. Paul was angry at life for denying him the bonus years of pleasure, but he didn't take it out on Mae. He simply went into quiet depression, which, to her, heralded the end of life.

Both women are determined to make the life they have left with these mates as fine a time as they possibly can.

If your mate becomes ill, here are some keys to coping with what life has handed you:

- Give of yourself to your loved one, but not to the extent of martyring yourself. In Juanelle's case, she found a woman who would sit with Norb and take care of his needs four hours each day. She applied for her old job and is back at the newspaper on a part-time basis. The money she makes pays for the caretaker and releases her to live a relatively normal life outside her home.

- Be cheerful when you're taking care of your mate, but not to the point of acting as if he's senile. I don't know why, but many nurses resort to a "we" when speaking to patients, as in "We are looking better today, aren't we?" Remember that there's still a man within that ailing body, and treat him as such. He's not a child to be pampered with platitudes.

- Give him the dignity of making choices. Don't plan a schedule so rigid that he feels he is institutionalized. For instance, why not a "Want your bath now or after we watch the news?" rather than "Bath time!"
- Do establish some pleasurable routines, such as watching the same TV programs each day. Try to make the viewings a mix of sitcoms and news. Keeping in contact with the outside world via the TV helps make your ailing one still feel part of that world. If it is possible, given his illness, discuss the news with him and try to engage in a dialogue.
- If there are children with grandchildren around, encourage them to visit, but not too long if they bring the tots. Little children are wearing on the healthiest of us, much less a sick person.
- Resume your own life as much as possible. Continue visiting with friends and attending meetings if you are club-minded. Perhaps you don't want to stay away as long as Juanelle, who went back to work, but do get away for a little bit each day. It will help you keep your perspective on the situation and make your husband feel that he is not a drag upon your existence.
- Do not let him make your life miserable with constant demands and recriminations. If he tries this—and many men do try to hold their wives' attention with constant requests for this, that and the other—simply tell him that you will do what you can when you can. Refusing to jump when he says "jump" will most likely tone down the commands.
- Begin a new hobby, even if it's one that you can do in an armchair by his bed. If you've never taken up handwork, such as knitting, embroidering or hand-quilting, go for it. Take lessons and report back to him what you're doing. Perhaps you've always had a yearning to paint. If possible, set up his sickbed in a well-lighted room and paint away where he can watch.

One wife knew her husband was rousing from his depression when he commented that she'd made the sky too blue in her seascape!

- Have someone outside the family to whom you can talk. This may be your minister or a good friend. If you have nobody, there are many support groups and agencies available that will help you learn to cope.

Take heart. Life may not have given you a fair deal, but with strength of character, compassion and love, you will learn to function within the boundaries of your situation.

15

PARTNERS IN BUSINESS, PARTNERS IN LIFE

Entering into retirement after you've spent years working in the same office with your mate may sound like the dullest of all retirement scenarios, but it need not be if you approach it with new and fresh ideas.

Bob and Bonnie met each other in first grade, dated through junior high school, and married after high school graduation. After his graduation from college, the two went into the insurance business together.

"After so many years in a high-pressure job situation, we were afraid that we would bore each other in retirement, but we made some changes in our lifestyle, and it's going to be fine," said Bonnie, a down-to-earth woman whose life has been devoted to family, home and business—in that order.

"We don't feel threatened by a full-time commitment, because that's what we have had for so many years," she continued. "There are no surprises in store for us because I've seen Bob in both a business and a personal life and he has seen me in both situations."

Neither will division of household labor cause friction in this household because the couple have been dividing chores for years.

However, Bonnie is clever enough to realize that after so many years of working together, something new must be put into the marriage at the time of retirement.

"We can't just do our homework and settle down to watch TV together. We've been very active and have worked hard. We are the kind of people who need to keep busy," she said.

During their work life, gregarious and enthusiastic Bob belonged to several service clubs and had been chairman for many projects. Since retirement, Bonnie has encouraged him to keep up with his service clubs and to put even more energy into club projects, because he now has the spare time.

Club work has never held fascination for Bonnie, although she has worked faithfully on the auxiliaries of Bob's clubs. Now that she's retired, she's happily busy with her favorite leisure-time activities—quilting and knitting. Because of her expertise in these crafts, she has found part-time work at a local yarn shop.

"We are both happy with our outside activities, and when we get together for dinner, we each have stories to tell about our day's happenings," Bonnie said.

Although you and your mate may have worked side by side for years, it is wise, during retirement, for both to get involved in outside projects, whether it is volunteer work like Bob's or a paying position like Bonnie's.

You and your spouse may not opt for the same solution that keeps Bob and Bonnie happy, but by putting your heads and your expertise together you can add a new and fresh dimension to your retirement years.

16

WHY DO WE NEED FRIENDS? WE HAVE OUR CHILDREN

The mother of a close friend actually made that remark about not seeking friendship because she had her children. Her daughter said to me, "Did you ever hear anything more chilling?"

She felt, and rightly so, that now the burden of providing a social life was squarely on her and her siblings and their children. No parent, she said, should ever put that weight on a child's shoulders even though the child is now a grownup.

Living your retired life through your children falls roughly into one of two categories:

—Regarding your children as your sole social life and seeking their company rather than making friends of your own.

—Allowing your children to run your social life by making irrationally exorbitant demands upon your time.

In Key 11, Fran and Wilbur fell into the first category. Remember how they sold their home and drove around the country in their RV, visiting each of five children during the entire year? They told themselves they were participating fully in their children's lives and would be remembered as loving parents.

The finale to this family togetherness came when Fran overheard a daughter-in-law say, "Get that woman out of my house. I don't care if she is your mother. She's driving me crazy."

Crushed, they departed the next day, wondering what they would do next. They enjoyed roaming around in an RV and, workaholics as they both were, they enjoyed keeping busy. They finally solved their problem by putting ads in publications of interest to RV and mobile home park owners. They would, their ad read, take over the managers' jobs for a certain amount of time. Receiving quite a few replies, they were able to select several parks in the areas where their children lived. In that way they would have a home base near the children for several weeks but wouldn't be in residence with them. Their excess fixer-up energy is now channeled into park projects.

But what if RVs don't figure in your retirement life? You're still in the family home and you are both retired. How can you tell if you're being a Parent Pest?

Take this test:

—Do you call your children more than once a day?

—Do you demand or whine to have them visit more than once a week?

—Do you insist that they give a major share of their free time to you?

—Do you invent tasks or errands that will take up their time?

If you answered yes to even one of these questions, you'd better take a look at your parenting skills. You are too demanding. Your children are functioning adults, and if you've been a loving parent they'll find their way to you.

The dumbest remark I ever heard a woman make was: "Well, if my parents didn't want to baby-sit, why did they have grandchildren?"

No, I didn't make that up. I was an *ear*-witness to the question. The obvious answer is that "I didn't make the grandchildren; you did," but that wouldn't have stopped this young woman who was determined to have her children and her social life, too.

Certainly you love your children, and you love their children, and taking care of those children—upon occasion—is a part of happy family life; but only in extreme circumstances should retired couples let themselves be taken for granted as unpaid child-care givers.

Take this little quiz:

—Do your children ask you to sit more than once every two weeks?

—Do your children emotionally bully you into child care with such statements as "If you don't take care of them, they won't know and love you"?

—Do your children take your baby-sitting as their God-given right?

—Do you feel guilty when you refuse your children's requests, whether for child care, money loans or other types of assistance?

When it comes to attempting to make your children your best friends, it is most often the wife who instigates this unhealthy closeness. A firm believer in "A mother is a mother is a mother . . .," she may find it difficult to separate her identity from that of her children. She may believe that if she doesn't baby-sit, the children will be left with uncaring sitters; therefore it is her duty to sit whenever requested. If she does not, she is an unfit grandmother, just as feared and heavy a burden as being an unfit mother.

If you answered yes to any of the questions in the preceding quiz, then you are being overused as a parent, and it's time to make your move toward a healthier relationship.

17

YOU MARRIED A WAY OF LIFE, AND NOW THAT'S ALL CHANGED?

For love or money or maybe a combination of both, many young women marry older men. When they are wed, the men are usually vital and energetic and a force in the marketplace. Then comes retirement, and suddenly a young woman finds herself with a full-time husband who is a good many years older.

The result can be disastrous, especially if there is little love and less compassion in the marriage. If there are these two vital ingredients, then there is hope for the older man/younger woman duo.

Sherrie was a 27-year-old red-haired beauty when she spotted Sam, a dynamic tycoon older than her own father. She decided that it was time to settle down, and she went after Sam with one purpose in mind.

Seven years later, the marriage seemed to be working out just fine. Whatever could go wrong?

Sam retired, that's what went wrong. He had sons ready to take over his business. Sherrie thought life would continue as usual with added perks such as more time for lengthy cruises, shopping sprees in foreign cities, and a constant round of parties and dinners. Instead, she found herself living with a man she didn't really know.

Sam felt old and, because you are as old as you feel, began acting like an old man. He was still infatuated with his young catch but not in exactly the same way as before. He became an angry, jealous man, watching the credit cards like the proverbial hawk and interrogating her as to her comings and goings. She retaliated with angry and hurtful put-downs regarding his age.

This marriage was on a downhill slide until Sherrie, a savvy woman who really loved her husband, went to a personal counselor. The counselor helped her realize that when a woman enters into marriage, be it for the man, the lifestyle, or both, this marriage is a partnership. Sam had kept his share of the partnership bargain. He provided Sherrie with his love, a good life and financial security. Her part of the bargain was to do everything within her power to keep him happy, healthy and contented.

For younger women who have married older men, Sherrie suggests asking these questions:

—Did your marriage take you out of a middle-class world into a life of wealth and ease? And did you consider this when you married this man?

—Are you 15 to 20 years younger than your husband?

—Would you have been attracted to and married this much older man if he'd been a supermarket checkout clerk?

—When entering into any friendship, are power and money your considerations?

There is no grade to this little quiz, but if you answered yes to any of the questions, you may be a woman who married a lifestyle. Let's hope you'll keep your part of the marriage contract by making your husband's retired life comfortable and happy, and that means a lot more than sex.

Sherrie's keys to turning an angry older retired husband into a friend as well as the lover she married are as follows:

• Don't be afraid to turn on the charm that attracted him to you in the first place. If you love this man, it's not demeaning to cuddle him and give him the strokes to bring him out of retirement despair.

- If money is no problem, use your imagination to keep him busy in plans for the future. There is an entire world to explore when fun funds are available.
- Even while you keep him occupied and happy, do remember that he is older and may be slowing down a bit. No need to wear him down as did Darlene, who picked her husband up from minor surgery at the hospital and took him straight to a cocktail party.
- If he's been busy tycooning and you've been busy social butterflying all your married life, now is the time to become his best friend. That means developing compatibility and mutual interests.
- Don't ever abuse the privilege of being a rich man's wife. Many a wife adapts so quickly to spending a man's money that he wonders what happened to that sweet and simple woman he married, the one who was so grateful for the gifts and trips. A woman who takes for granted all that her husband gives her is not a loving wife.

Maybe you were interested in this man's way of life instead of the man himself when you married him, but that needn't mean you're any less of a wife now if you help him find happiness in his retired years.

18

WE'RE STILL NEWLYWEDS: HOW DO WE HANDLE RETIREMENT?

The positive answer to that question is that you're in the very best of circumstances to enjoy retirement. As newlyweds, you have only a short history together and are still exploring the wonderful world of marriage. In retirement, you will have freedom from many responsibilities, hopefully you will have economic stability and you will appreciate the good fortune of having found each other.

Before or just after retirement, you two should sit down and discuss the following items:

1. What grand new options and experiences you're going to explore now that you have the time.
2. Problems that may arise and how you can work to solve them.
3. Ways in which you can help and support your mate's private dreams and hobbies.

Item (1). The sky is the limit now for adventures that you two haven't had the time or energy to enjoy while you were working. This is the time to begin joint projects. One new wife was amazed to find that her husband had little or no idea, beyond his grandfather's name, where his family had sprung from. They took a class in genealogy and began exploring his family tree via microfilmed old newspapers in the town where his grandfather had lived and died. The obituary, written in fine old turn-of-the-century style, gave them a set of clues to follow.

"It was more fun than any detective story we ever watched on TV, and gave my husband a great sense of self that he'd never had before. He was delighted to find his grandfather described as a 'fine and upstanding member of his community and a man who would be sorely missed,' " said the new wife.

Having gotten the grandfather's place of birth from the obituary, they are off and traveling to Kentucky, where they hope to find out even more about the family.

Another couple purchased a copy of historical geographical names for their particular state. They explore constantly, discovering old town sites long forgotten.

"All those things you've wanted to do but haven't had time for are now yours for the taking," said a newly wed and newly retired woman. "And the most wonderful thing in the world is to wake up in the morning and know that you have someone to do these things with you."

Item (2). One problem might be the discovery of annoying little habits in your mate that you didn't notice before retirement. Perhaps he has also discovered some things you do that bother him. Discussions tempered with humor and tolerance can help solve these minor irritations.

Another problem might be that of children from previous marriages. One wife discovered to her dismay that her husband's grown children regarded his retirement as an open invitation to hang out at the family home, with free baby-sitting for their little ones expected as their rightful dues.

Her husband was delighted that his children and grandchildren enjoyed his company, and the second wife enjoyed having them, too—up to a point. However, her fuse shortened when she realized that their home, which had been *his* home before their wedding, was rapidly becoming a hotel. Her many hints about calling "before you come over" were ignored, and her temper flared. Only by stating her case for privacy firmly, with both children and husband present so no tales could be embellished through retelling, was she able to solve this very real problem.

Item (3). Your partner may have personal retirement dreams that you, as a newlywed, are not yet privy to. Take the case of Rose and Jerry. They had been married only four years before Jerry retired. Since Rose was in a profession where much of her work could be done at home, the couple enjoyed a wonderful second honeymoon until she began fretting over the lack of productivity in her writing.

"Enough of this little stuff," she said. "I'm ready to write a book now."

So she settled down to do so. Anybody who has done some writing knows that it is a demanding and lonely activity. If you're not actually writing, you're thinking about what you're going to write.

Jerry, a most understanding husband, wanted to help her make her dream come true. He worked with her to create a writing space, then backed off and let her go to it. Rather than demand attention from her, he got busy on his own projects.

Realizing how fortunate she was, Rose learned to schedule her writing so that she had time to prepare meals and finish her household chores, while still leaving time to talk and cuddle with her understanding and wonderful husband.

If you work together at solving problems as they arise, if you share the freedom and fun, and if you help each other work at realizing dreams, retirement can be the second honeymoon you've been waiting for.

19

THE BIG TAKEOVER: WHO'S THE BOSS HERE?

It's lamentable that, even in a company of two, there needs to be a boss. There's no surprise in this—pecking orders have been around since the world began. However, if your usually amenable husband is assuming a strong "This is your captain speaking . . . " manner after retirement, there is a reason. He may be feeling the need to recoup the agreeable sensation of being in control again—even at the expense of hurting your feelings.

It may be necessary for you to change the habits of a lifetime, but because you two are going to spend so much more time together than ever before, it will save a lot of anger and anguish if you establish—early in a retirement—a partnership rather than a corporation consisting of one boss and one employee.

How best can you accomplish this? Head-on bluntness may turn the trick, but this tactic is almost guaranteed to create friction. A softer approach is a happier and longer-lasting solution.

Here's how Madge solved the problem.

Until Mort's retirement, Mort and Madge were a well-adjusted couple in the old-fashioned way. He had fulfilled the role of provider; she had fulfilled the role of homemaker, although she did work part-time at a pharmacy. Madge decided to retire when Mort did so that they could enjoy retirement.

The first few months went really very well. Mort rearranged one bedroom in their large old Victorian home as an office, and Madge went happily about her usual rounds.

Nothing to this retirement, she thought contentedly, until the day that the refrigerator went on the fritz and she was warned by the repairman that the condition would soon be terminal.

She told Mort the bad news. He brightened. A project! Immediately he set out for the supermarket and bought all the consumer magazines he could find; then he sat down to study the best buys in refrigerators.

Within a week, he remarked one morning that he was off to buy a new appliance. Madge said, "Hold it. We'll go together to buy a new one." After a moment's silence, he agreed, and they set out for the appliance department of a large store.

A salesman approached Mort, asking if he could help. "I'm in the market for a refrigerator," said Mort, and away the two of them went, leaving Madge to trail behind. After thirty minutes of comparison shopping, Mort said to Madge, "We'll take this one."

Madge said, "I don't really like that one. The shelves must have been designed by a man who hates wives who clean refrigerators. It may be energy saving, but it would be a bear to clean. I prefer the first one we looked at."

Mort puffed up like a blowfish. He turned to the salesman and said, "I'll be back later." Not "we," but "I."

Once in the car, he began to lecture Marge on how women should leave the buying of appliances to men because men have a much greater grasp of mechanical fundamentals—and, besides, hadn't he done all that studying?

Something snapped within easygoing Madge, and she let loose with a diatribe on Mort's high-handed attitude toward her in the store. Her rage went past the immediate and into the past. Soon the car was filled with recriminatory and destructive phrases.

For several days, the temperature in the Mort/Madge dwelling was cooler than that inside the ailing refrigerator. Mort rumbled around lonesomely in his workshop, lower lip protruding in a pout. Madge rattled around in her kitchen, rearranging her spice rack. Mealtimes were the only togetherness periods, and the togetherness was represented only by an occasional "Pass the potatoes."

Neither was happy during this unplanned-for separation, and both realized that this was no way to begin the rest of their lives together.

Madge, who truly loved her husband, made the first move. A thinker-out of problems, she realized that she must begin to mend the breach, but before she kissed and made up she had to map out her plan.

Any true believer in star signs can tell you that Virgos are super-organized people and like to make lists. A Virgo to her logical fingertips, Madge sat down to make a list outlining the past few days.

Her first entry was, "The refrigerator incident is only a symptom of the problem; it is not the problem."

She was right. Mort's takeover of the appliance purchase was a manifestation of his insecurity. By attempting to maintain control over Madge's purchasing power, Mort felt he had a semblance of control over his household. He might no longer be El Supremo in firm control of the state highway division's purchasing department, but, by God, he could buy one refrigerator.

He believes he isn't in control of anything except me, Madge realized. What a frightening thought, she said to herself, filled with compassion for her big, husky husband who was now, in his own mind, a diminished man.

The second entry on her list was, "How can I make the situation better right now?" and the next was, "How can I prevent this kind of conflict in the future?"

The answer came quickly to this intuitive woman. First, she had to soothe the savage beast banging around in the workshop. Abandoning her usual modest approach, she went out to the workshop, put her arms around Mort and said, "Come into the house. I want to talk to you—in bed."

Now, don't laugh. Mort may have been so taken aback that he couldn't answer, but he could move right up the stairs! And she made a startling discovery about herself. She found that sexual aggressiveness turned her on. The result was a glorious lovemaking session such as they hadn't enjoyed for years.

Obviously, sex is not the answer to every midlife problem, but in this case the resultant closeness gave Madge the opportunity to state her case quietly but firmly.

What she said to her husband, who was now in the mood to listen, was:

"I love you very much and I don't want us to spend the rest of our lives fighting for supremacy. Let's make a treaty. You have your areas of expertise. I have mine. I'll respect yours if you respect mine. Let's begin making decisions together."

This wasn't the last time Mort tried his El Supremo routine, of course, but nowadays when he sounds off, Madge is savvy enough to put her arms around him and say, "Hey, remember the treaty we made?"

There is no longer a boss and an employee in their household. There are just two people who have learned to work out problems with love and discussion.

20

TERRITORIAL STRIFE AND HOW TO AVOID IT

One of the most often-voiced complaints I hear from wives is: "He's always in my way. Wherever I need to be, he seems to be right there. How can I avoid this territorial strife? It's driving me nuts."

The first thing you must do is get a grip on yourself and realize one very important fact: It's his house, too. He may have been out of this house for a good part of every day for years, but now he is retired. This is his territory as much as yours. Learning to live with this and with each other is easier said than done. Where you live does make a difference.

Whit and Susan sold their big family home and moved into a sleek new condominium with vaulted ceilings, loads of closet space and state-of-the-art appliances.

"Every morning I wake up and think, 'What am I doing in this Hollywood heaven?' " asked Susan, a commonsense woman who'd raised four children while Whit was busy as a traveling salesman. "It makes me happy to look at the beauty of this place, but trying to live in it with Whit under my feet is driving me batty. He can only play golf so long—he has to come home sometime, poor guy—but when I get all my patterns and sewing spread out and he comes tromping in, my heart sinks."

For Susan and Whit, the answer to space was relatively simple. They converted the second bedroom from a guest room to a den for Whit, complete with built-in bookshelves, a large desk and a TV for his sports-viewing pleasure.

This was a simple and easy conversion for these two, but it was simple because Susan had the compassion and the fairness to realize that Whit needed some breathing room, too.

On the other hand, Ellen and Bob had a similar living arrangement, but Ellen was clinging to what she termed "my space" with grim and not-so-loving determination. When Bob decided he'd like to take up cooking, he was squashed like a bug by Ellen, who threatened, "Not in my kitchen, you don't."

At last check, Bob's portion of their spacious apartment is an easy chair and a hassock in the living room. When he returns home from errands, he goes right to his chair.

"Reminds me of a well-trained dog," said a man who deplores Ellen's territorial dominance.

Ellen herself is getting a little grouchy. Seems Bob is spending more and more time down at the Elks Club. And why shouldn't he? His wife hasn't made it comfortable for him at home.

So when you two begin getting under each other's feet and into each other's hair, take a look at what you are doing to make the home situation workable. Not all men are able to look around a living space and decide what should be done to make it livable for both.

Some hints from wives who have lived to laugh about territorial strife:

- Establish a routine as soon as possible after retirement. If you know roughly where the other is going to be at a certain time, you can change your traffic pattern to steer clear.
- Privacy is important. If you've been using just one bathroom in the master bedroom because he's been at work most of the day, put the guest bathroom into use, said one wife, who graciously gave over the big

bathroom to her husband and took the smaller one for herself. "There's more bathroom privacy for each of us this way."

- Moved to smaller living space where there's no longer a man-sized den? Make your living room a comfort zone even if it means giving up the spiffy French Provincial white furniture you've always loved.
- Enlist your husband's aid in creating extra space for his needs and hobbies. In addition to making him feel needed and loved, this will give him a project. Many men love projects!
- If you're lucky enough to have a husband who does want to try his hand at cooking, as did poor Bob before Ellen rained on his culinary parade, let him experiment as often as he wants. If there's nutmeg on the chicken-fried steak, so be it. He's trying and he's busy, isn't he?

Creating a stress-free living environment is going to depend a lot on your attitude. Three things to remember: Be kind. Be fair. And above all, be a loving, compassionate wife who wants to make life comfortable for her husband.

21

MODEST BUDGETS NEED NOT LIMIT PLEASURES

Elise and Phil were Depression Era children. They remember cold winters and hard times. Even after they moved to California from North Dakota at the end of World War II and found good-paying jobs, the couple could never relax about spending money for fun. The remembrance of tough times was too vivid for them to splurge.

But in no way were this couple dull and boring. They had many friends and enjoyed good times, but just didn't like spending too much money on pleasure.

After they both retired, they rattled around for a few months in their big house, eventually finding volunteer and social activities that pleased them. Money wasn't a problem but neither was it particularly plentiful. They lived on the interest of their savings, their individual retirement plans and their Social Security.

"Maybe while we were working we should have spent more money on fun," said Elise, who has always wanted to travel. "But if we had, then we wouldn't have as steady an income as we do. Things cost so much now."

Because of their frugal leanings, Phil and Elise are masters at having fun for little or no money, and their methods can be a textbook for those living on adequate but fixed incomes.

In many cases, it is the wife who plans the "social" aspects of life either before or after retirement, and Elise was no different. The first thing she initiated with Phil was a discussion of their monthly budget to figure out how much they have to spend on fun. They set up a "fun box" for monthly recreation, and opened an interest-bearing bank account for their long-range travel fund.

Elise found the following bargains, some specifically for seniors, to enrich their daily social life and pleasures at minimal cost:

No-cost fun. Elise began researching the Arts and Entertainment section of her newspaper for concerts, lectures, discussions and workshops available to seniors.

She and Phil took up "mall meandering" as a social outing. Many seniors find fun and exercise walking through the malls in their city or town. Some seniors even have a one- or two-mile walk paced off and, during bad weather, take their daily walk in the mall. At the conclusion of the walk, they may stop for coffee and muffins at a mall bakery. Watch your local paper for mall happenings because there is often great entertainment offered for no cost.

Little-or-no-cost fun. Elise checked the entertainment or club calendar of her local newspaper daily and found events such as movie matinees and community college plays for low prices. Through careful perusal, Elise and Phil have attended a Bach recital at a local college, seen a dress-rehearsal of *Hello, Dolly!* for free at the city's little theater and participated in folk dancing at a local church group.

She cajoled Phil into visiting the senior center with her to check into the activities there. They found that most centers have birthday parties, dances, card parties and socials for little or next to nothing. And the centers are a nice place to meet couples with similar interests.

Elise joined an art guild that was responsible for hanging and exhibiting local artists' works in a performance center/art gallery complex. Members have the opportunity to usher at the theater during performances, and their spouses get in for half price. Elise has met some fascinating people and formed lasting friendships, while also enjoying the performances with Phil.

Coupon clipping. This is the day of the coupon, and there are coupons for practically every type of goods or services plus entertainment. Since dining out was a special treat for Elise, she checked newspapers, her own mailbox and shopper publications for coupons for dinners and lunches. When a local service club sold entertainment books that offered bargains on motels, meals and entertainment, she bought one.

She and Phil dine out once a week on "twofers" (two for one coupons), and have enjoyed a variety of ethnic cuisines, good old American fast food, and even more elaborate dinners offered through "Dine Early and Save" coupons from more expensive restaurants.

As Elise said, things do cost more now, but there are always free or inexpensive good times to be had if a fixed-income couple will do some detective work. For information on travel price breaks for seniors, turn to the next key.

22

TRAVEL FOR RETIRED FOLKS? IT'S NEVER BEEN EASIER

Even the most depressed of retired husbands will usually respond to an enthusiastic "Let's take a trip!" suggestion from a loving wife. He'll be so busy with travel plans he won't have time to miss the old gang and certainly not the confining routine of the workplace.

One tip from a human relations expert: Don't shoot your entire year's travel budget on a big trip which begins immediately after retirement. The reason? When it's over, you're back home again with no plans for the future and little to look forward to. Better to retire, take six months to work together on travel plans, then head out. When you get back, you'll have your retirement routine pretty much worked out and you'll be delighted to be home again, ready to plan the next jaunt.

Financial situation has a lot to do with the when and where you'll go, but if you have a fixed and tight budget, take heart. Seniors are right up there next to students and teachers when it comes to travel, and travel-related industries vie for your business. The result is that travel for retired folks has never been easier or more affordable, no matter what kind of travel you desire.

And what are your aims? Will you be:

Trippers interested in taking daily or short overnight drives to nearby places of interest? Read carefully the travel section of your newspapers each week to discover often-overlooked places of interest in your own state.

Service organizations often sell entertainment books that offer discount coupons on food and lodging in your state. Take advantage of these and plan your trips accordingly.

Nomadic RV campers who roam from state to state taking in the sights of America first? A word of caution here: Unless you've experienced a lot of life on the open road and are an especially gregarious woman who makes new friends easily, don't let your husband persuade you to sell your home base and live out your days on wheels.

Men seem to take to nomadic life more easily than do their wives, said one woman whose husband talked her into this life. "I've missed my children, my friends and my home more than I ever expected to. The night we called home and found we'd missed the premature birth of a grandchild was the night I fell apart and asked to be taken home. Thank goodness, we'd kept our house. It took us some time to regain our home from the tenants, but it was worth the trouble. Now we just crank up the RV two or three times a year. When we travel now, I really look forward to it."

If you are not already a member of an auto club, this might be a good time to join, whether you are a quick tripper or an RV roamer. Once you've decided on a destination, your travel club adviser can help plan your trip. Club personnel will provide you with a personalized travel routing to your destination, maps and, in some instances, tour books that include lists of accommodations, car rental agencies, restaurants and points of interest in the areas you will be visiting. Your adviser usually can make lodging and car rental reservations for you. Eligible club members can receive senior citizen discounts at many of the places.

Don't be timid about asking for lodging discounts. On a recent trip, I asked the rate at a new motel, was told the amount and said, "No, thank you." The clerk said, "Well, what would you pay?" I named a figure, to which she agreed. We got the room for $18 less than the amount I was first quoted.

Large-scale travelers with the world as your oyster? There are more trip savings available to seniors now than ever before. For flight savings, one travel agent I know recommends coupon booklets. Almost every major airline offers these booklets, which can be purchased through your travel agents or from individual airlines. Prices differ from carrier to carrier, but at the time this book was written, coupon booklets were about $500 for four coupons on two round trips, $800 for eight coupons or four round trips to anywhere the airline flies. Alaska and Hawaii often are exempt.

For the folks who are new to travel, many agents advise taking a cruise. The price is inclusive, and a cruise is a worry-free way to enjoy your first major trip. There are prices for most budgets.

Escorted tours are also a good way to ease into a traveling life. On both the cruise and the escorted tour, the traveler never need worry about where he will lay his head that night or whether he will have to haul luggage up and down the stairs, or what the menu will be. This is all planned and paid for ahead, although on escorted tours there are a few free nights for dinner or optional side trips which cost extra.

For all trips, be sure to ask for the 10 percent discount which is given to seniors over 62 and their companions, even though the companion may be under 62.

Elderhostel, in existence now for 15 years, is a wonderful way for seniors (one party must be 60 or over, the other at least 50) to see and experience the United States as well as foreign countries. These learning vacations for seniors provide simple accommodations at modest costs, frequently in college or university dorms.

The typical charge for a six-night program at sites in almost every state in the U.S. is $275, $295 (U.S. currency) in Canada. Alaska or Hawaii may cost slightly more. This price includes meals, lodging, side trips and academic classes. International travel naturally costs more.

In 1990, the Elderhostel program served 215,000 seniors, up from 190,000 in 1989. These trips offer hundreds of study programs at scores of sites, and the classes, no larger than 50, are designed for every interest. There are no educational barriers. You can be an eighth-grade graduate or the holder of a PhD. Each state has an Elderhostel director, and Elderhostel catalogs (fascinating reading!) are available upon request by writing Elderhostel, 75 Federal Street, Boston, MA 02110.

Whether your travel is on a limited or a grand scale, there is no better way for a retired couple to broaden their horizons and add zest to their new life.

23

SMOTHER LOVE AND HOW TO GET OUT FROM UNDER

One of the sweetest and gentlest women I've ever known was the most brainwashed woman I've ever met, and she never had a clue as to what was being done to her. It was a difficult thing for me to watch as we worked together every evening in a small office.

For me, the evening work was the culmination of a long and busy day, while her shift began at four in the afternoon. Around 5:30, the phone calls began. They were from Carl, her retired husband. Never a pleasant man to be around when he descended on the office, he displayed even worse phone manners, and the calls grew more and more demanding and abusive as the evening wore on.

I could usually tell by the answers what the questions were:

"Just look in the oven. You'll find a nice stew."

"The napkins are on the table."

"But I did do that."

"I'll be home at 12:08, just like always."

"Yes, I remembered to . . ."

It was difficult for me to listen to this lovely woman of 62 respond so nervously and defensively to Carl's demands and recriminations.

When I finally got up enough courage to ask Grace why she allowed herself to be hounded so much while she was trying to work—her job was very detailed and required lots of concentration—she answered with a smile on her lips and love in her voice:

"He loves me so much that he just can't seem to get along without me, especially now that he's retired," she would say with a pleased smile after a particularly long phone call.

More like tyranny than love, I thought, and a fine method of control over Grace. Carl knew well his wife's passive temperament, and his bullying tactics were just one more power play for this unpleasant man.

Although Grace evidently had lived with this for years, control under the guise of smother love is new and worrying for some wives of newly retired husbands. Men who attempt to control women, under the protection of true love, often use one of these two methods:

Weakness. "I can't handle it without you here. Don't leave me alone too long. I'm so lonely. I love you so much, I can't be away from you too long. I don't know what I'd do without you." These are some of the phrases wives report hearing far too often.

Blustering or cruel accusations. This was Carl's MO. He constantly had poor Grace on the defensive, certain that somehow it was her fault he could not get along without her.

Whatever the method, wives often wind up feeling guilty. Wives who have worked their way through this problem offer advice for women who are being harassed under the guise of love:

- Do not react when he verbally hits you with a "who, what, when, where, why and how" interrogation. Simply remain quiet until the blast is over, then answer—briefly—where you've been. Don't offer any excuses or get defensive.
- If you are still employed and your job calls for you to attend functions, or you simply want to do some-

thing with friends, go right ahead with your plans. His retirement does not your prison make. If he rages and rants, let him. You don't need his permission.

- If you're an at-home wife, go about the activities that interest you. Don't let his bullying or whining intimidate you into denying your own pleasures. On the other hand, don't overdo your outside activities. He may have a legitimate gripe if you're so busy you don't have any time for him.

- If the situation gets so bad that you simply can't stand the pressure, don't be afraid to go on the assertive. Wait until he's quiet, look him in the eye and say, "Your bullying actions are causing me much unhappiness. My life cannot and should not solely revolve around your wishes now that you are retired. It is becoming difficult for me to want to come home. I would like our life together to be happy and without pressure. How shall we go about making it better?"

A simple declaration and questioning of this type often will defuse the most belligerent of men.

If the talk does no good, you have several options including (1) going for counseling, (2) getting out of the marriage or (3) going about your business without letting his browbeating tactics get under your skin—tough to do, but it may pay off if you're strong enough to take it.

A last word from a woman who freed herself from love tyranny: "Don't let yourself be mentally shoved around. You are only as guilty as you allow him to make you feel."

24

HE'S NEVER DEVELOPED HOBBIES: HOW CAN I HELP HIM?

Webster's New World Dictionary of the American Language defines a hobby as "something that a person likes to do or study in his spare time, a favorite pastime or avocation." Because your husband has been so busy working, maybe he's never had the time to pursue a hobby other than an occasional round of social golf. But now, in the retirement years, there is plenty of spare time, and an engrossing hobby may be just the ticket for your mate. Don't decide for him which one he'd like. Force-feeding doesn't encourage enthusiasm. But there are ways a wife can encourage her husband and make him aware of the many possibilities that exist.

There were Madge and Mort, who became interested in Western dancing on a little sightseeing trip she had planned to a cowtown in their state; now they have a hobby to enjoy together. And there was the wife who became fascinated with her husband's ancestors and now he's as avid a genealogist as she is. These women didn't set out to find hobbies for their husbands. It just happened. Neither of these men had had hobbies before being exposed to the world that existed outside full-time work.

In the olden days, as my children are wont to call my youth, there wasn't as much for retired people to do. Most of them spent a lot of time at home, gardened, listened to the radio, attended their house of worship on weekends, and socialized with family and friends.

Maybe the husband went fishing occasionally. Maybe the wife quilted or worked with her woman's club or lodge.

Today's retired couples may be approximately the same age as yesterday's, but with the vast amount of information fed us, today's retirees are often light-years younger in thoughts and interests than were their parents. Health permitting, there are few limitations to the fun a retired couple can have in recreational pursuits.

Before you and your husband embark on an interest—either solo or in tandem—there are things to consider. Will this be a hobby pursued basically at home or one where much away time is necessary? Either can have drawbacks. Do you want a hobby in which you can both be involved? Shared interests can do much to perk up any marriage—whether or not the couple are retired. Or maybe you each need some alone time, and a solo hobby would be more appropriate. These are decisions to be made by you and your spouse.

How can a wife help her husband develop hobby interests?

1. Listen to what he's saying.
2. Look at what he reads.
3. Watch to see what interests him.

Listen to what he's saying. Julia helped Ernie become interested in a hobby by using the listening technique. On their walks, Ernie complained constantly about the rose garden at a nearby park. It wasn't quite up to the standard he thought it should be, considering that their hometown was advertised as the City of Roses. Julia listened closely, then called the city parks department. Were there any volunteer positions open for rose lovers? Well, yes, there was a group of volunteer gardeners, the director said. When Julie asked if Ernie would be interested, he quickly agreed, and as a result joined the city's volunteer gardening group. This put him in touch with a local rose society, whose members share rose-tending tips, crossbreed varieties, and put on rose shows and competitions.

Julia had listened and Ernie profited.

Look at what he reads. Stan had always been an avid reader, anything he could get his hands on. The couple had two newspapers delivered to their home each day, and Stan read each from cover to cover. After retirement, he read even more. When the local morning paper ran a notice asking for interested citizens to sit in on editorial board meetings, Kathryn called Stan's attention to it and he applied for the position. He was accepted and enjoyed the sessions. The editorial board stint has spun off into a study group of men who are interested in community government and civic improvement. He is now a busy and involved man.

Notice what interests him. Nola complained one day that a table top had gotten scratched in a pitched battle between two young grandchildren. How could she minimize the scratch? Ole began trying different home remedies for wounded wood and succeeded in reducing the scratch to a barely visible mark.

Then Nola hauled home a vintage office chair to go with an old rolltop desk they had. They would go together perfectly, she said of her garage sale purchase. Ole wasn't enthusiastic at first, but soon she noticed that he was poking around the garage for wood glue and clamps. The next day, he was deep into restoration of the chair.

Now on their drives they stop at secondhand stores and garage sales. When they find an interesting piece of furniture, they lug it home. Nola sands and Ole does the refinishing. They're having fun and making a little money in resales on the side. (Look to your own skills and interests, because cottage industries are definitely possible after retirement.)

Hobbies are as diverse as are the people who pursue them. They can be as simple as working crossword puzzles or collecting baseball cards; as creative as making wooden toys for Christmas sales or designing stained glass windows. A hobby need take you no farther than your armchair, although one that gets you out and involved is especially beneficial to a retired person.

Hobbies are exactly what a person makes of them, and a well-pursued hobby can lift you and your husband right out of the retirement blues.

25

VOLUNTEERING: THE ANSWER FOR MANY MEN

Helping others may be one of life's most rewarding deeds, but sometimes it's tough to persuade a man who's worked all his life for pay to work for free. Retirement-age men often have preconceived ideas about volunteering, because in past years it has been the women who have donated countless hours to volunteer service. Sure, men coached Little League teams and Peanut Basketball squads, worked on service-club related projects or served on boards, but volunteerism has traditionally been a homemaker's off-duty activity.

Times have changed, and it is becoming increasingly common for men, especially retirees, to give service without pay to their community.

"When a man retires, he has three choices," says one perceptive retiree. "He can retire to have fun. He can retire and give back to the community in which he lives. Or he can have a mix of both, which is nice for everyone concerned."

But what if your husband balks at the idea of "getting out there and stuffing envelopes with a bunch of chatty women"? The first thing you must do is convince him that in today's world, there are countless ways to serve without stuffing envelopes, although there are plenty of envelopes to be stuffed and sealed and somebody is going to have to do it.

Bill was one who balked at volunteerism because he thought it involved sit-down office work. Then his wife,

Sylvia, discovered that there was a wood-cutting crew from their church. The men cut wood during the summer months to give to needy families for their wood-burning heaters during the cold months. Another church needed drivers for a city-sponsored Meals on Wheels program. At her urging, Bill investigated and found friends in both projects. An outdoorsman all of his life, Bill now heads the wood-cutting crew and has never missed a day delivering hot meals for needy shut-ins.

If your husband is a doer, the idea of volunteering is enough to get him started on his own. If he's a procrastinator and has no idea of volunteer jobs available, help him by checking with your local Volunteer Exchange Bureau if there is one. If not, state and federal agencies, local churches and service clubs will be delighted to list their needs.

Here are some ways to serve:

Veterans hospitals. Chances are your husband is a veteran of World War II or the Korean War. VA hospitals are a perfect place for a man to help out. Sometimes just sitting and swapping combat tales with an old vet can make the day for both. Either you or your husband can call the nearest veterans hospital and ask to speak to the volunteer coordinator or equivalent.

Children with special needs. If he's good with the grandchildren, he may be good with others' children. There are countless ways to help needy children. One contact is your state's Human Resources Division, an agency that works with disadvantaged, abused or foster children. Your own church or your city's schools and public library also are likely places for volunteer jobs involving children. Emotionally disturbed teens often benefit from a male viewpoint. Some training might be needed for these volunteer services, but they are especially rewarding.

Literacy volunteer agencies. These agencies, which help adults learn to read, especially need male volunteers. What a joy it is to open up new worlds for these people!

Your local senior center. Senior centers generally have several paid staffers but rely mainly on volunteer expertise for most programs, and this is a good way to get both of you involved as a couple in volunteer work.

Whatever has been a man's skill in the workplace, there is a place in the volunteer world that would welcome and value his expertise and talent.

26

HE'S RETIRED AND OUT OF THE HOUSE—IS HE OUT OF YOUR LIFE?

The hoopla is over, you're ready to settle in for retirement, but you can't find him. He's already out the door, clubs slung over his shoulder and the car headed for the golf course. Maybe he's not a golfer but a fisherman, and the rod's packed and the smelly bait has mercifully been removed from your freezer.

You're alone, and you thought you were going to be a real twosome again as you were during your courtship days.

Don't despair if your mate falls into the category of Disappearing Husband in the months after retirement. This may well reflect a mentally healthy man who will eventually learn to slow down and take retirement in stride.

It is the man with a definite plan (even though many women don't consider golfing or fishing a planned occupation) who is best off after retirement. He has somewhere to go and something to do. The fact that it is a healthy sign should brighten your days even if you are feeling a bit neglected. Roll with it for a time, anyway. Let him go his way, enjoy his freedom. There are some suggestions about ways to bring him home again later in this key.

Many men build up retirement fantasies in their minds. They're going to improve their golf game. Or catch every fish in the stream. Or grow the best vegetable garden. Or sail or ski to their heart's content.

These fantasies are healthy if they are relatively realistic. They are only dangerous when a retiree aspires to young men's physical sports to prove he's still a macho fellow.

I remember such a man who decided, with no physical preparation, to take up cross-country skiing again after years at a sedentary desk job. He just put on skis, grabbed his poles and away he went, mile after grueling mile. "I'm punishing myself for getting so far out of shape," he told everyone. What happened to this foolish fellow? He was dead of a massive coronary within a short period of time, I'm sorry to say. His 59-year-old widow is trying to put her life back together because she blames herself for not trying to slow him down.

Could she have stopped him? Not easily, because some retired men feel an overwhelming need to prove themselves. She might have tried a serious talk with him with other family members present, or she might have enlisted the aid of the family doctor. If your husband decides he's going to take up a physically demanding sport, try intervention with either or both of these suggestions. A few tears and "I love you and want you around" pleas won't hurt, either.

Let's return to the man who isn't after punishing sports, but just seems to be heading for a retirement that doesn't include you.

Janelle, a working wife and a former golf widow, offers some tips for the "always with the fellows" type of husband.

- Sit down and discuss a division-of-labor plan with him. You're happy to let him live out his fantasies, but he must share the household load. Appeal to his sense of fairness, but don't let him off the hook if his gaze starts drifting toward the door, says Janelle. Let him know you mean business.
- If you are working five days a week, as was Janelle,

don't complain about his daytime away-from-home hobbies if he's pulling his share of the chore load. Do tell him that you'd appreciate his company after your work hours and his play hours. Explain why you feel that being away from home every night playing cards is not acceptable husband behavior.

- It is reasonable to expect to spend time together on the weekends. Although Janelle was home weekends, Mick still kept up his disappearing act to the golf course. He would spend both Saturday and Sunday playing golf; then after a round, he and his friends would have a few drinks and play some gin rummy. He'd drag home about five o'clock and collapse in his chair after asking what was on the dinner menu. Keeping her anger under control, Janelle decided to propose a compromise. They would do the weekend chores together Saturday morning. He could have one weekend afternoon off—Saturday or Sunday, his choice. Whether it was family day with the children, or a drive to the coast or maybe golf together, the rest of the time was going to be a Janelle-and-Mick duo. Mick, a fair fellow, agreed that the idea was sensible, and now the two have great weekends.

Janelle maintains she has discovered the real key to keeping a husband home. She says her recipe is to add a little spice to their life by being quietly mysterious about where she's been while he's gone. Plus knowing that plenty of good loving and good cooking is waiting for him when he gets home will bring even the most avid hunter home from the hill—or golfer home from the links.

When she retires in a few years, Janelle knows that they will need to sit down and work out a new plan that allows each partner free time while still providing plenty of time for each other to share activities.

The compulsive desire for such activities as golf or fishing—the "retirement honeymoon period," as one retirement planning counselor calls it—usually lasts about six months; then most husbands cast about for other things to do. And that's where you come in with all the good ideas you've been storing up.

27

MONEY, MONEY: WHO'S GOT THE MONEY?

By the time retirement rolls around, most couples have their financial plans worked out. For this book I interviewed a number of women to determine who manages the finances in retirement. There were nearly as many methods as there were couples!

I found:

—One couple working out of one checkbook, the wife complaining loudly that whenever she needed to make a purchase, the checkbook was with her husband. Presumably, the husband had the same complaint. At last report, this eccentric couple was planning to get two checkbooks for the same account. I hope they communicate well with each other. This could prove to be an explosive and costly experiment.

—Women who are handed a weekly or monthly allowance in the amount their husbands have decided they need. Passive wives—generally longtime wives who went right from their parents' home to their husbands'—meekly accepted this because it "has always been this way." More outspoken wives and working wives often balked at this restraint, which they considered humiliating.

"I'm a little too old for my husband to hand me money for being a good girl," said one wife who had been in this situation for years. When asked why she hadn't made a stand, she sighed and said, "I just want to keep peace in the family."

—Women who handled all the money and doled it out to husbands when needed. Not too many in this category. Most men like to have a say in money matters.

—Several marriages in which the wife paid the household bills while the husband handled the investments and payment of property and income taxes.

—Many marriages where there were "his," "hers" and "household" accounts. Truly the most sensible situation, said most of these wives. "When we get our retirement checks, we decide how much money we need for bills and how much goes into savings. The rest we divvy up and put into our separate accounts."

—One woman who never worried about household accounts, but kept her own Social Security check as her mad money.

Most women were content with the way finances were handled, but there were some areas of conflict. Following are some problems and possible solutions suggested by women who have survived these money questions:

—A working woman who is asked to hand over her check to a retired husband. After paying the household bills, he hands her back whatever he deems necessary for her expenses. Many newly married working women dislike this method and suggest that the most sensible solution is to establish at least two accounts: an account for his spending money and the household expenses, and an account for her, so that she feels she has partial control over her earnings.

Many longtime-married working wives say they put their check into the couple's joint account and take what they need. "Just don't overdo it when you get a raise. That isn't fair," says one.

If a longtime-married woman decides she wants separate accounts, there may be a battle, warns one woman who entered the workplace later in life and ended up with a high-paying job. Becoming weary of handing over her check, she had what she considered a rational discussion with her husband about having her own checking account. Wham! She was greeted with a tirade of refusals to consider this. She finally ended up going to the bank and opening her own account.

"After I'd done this, I went home and said, 'I've opened my own checking account. I'm willing to pay my fair share of the household bills. Now, either I can give you a check for what you feel you'll need or you can give me some bills to pay myself. It is your choice, Nathan, so you decide.' "

Some husbands are into control and what better way, they figure, than by divine right of the pocketbook.

—A woman who has no income of her own other than what her husband chooses to give her. Wives like this are in a poor bargaining position. They may establish an embargo on maid and chef services, and even sex, but these are poor ways of handling such a situation. Most wives interviewed agreed that if this situation becomes intolerable, these women should seek professional counseling.

—A wife who has taken care of all the bills during her husband's working years, only to have him demand the accounts the second week after retirement. From now on, he'll tend the family finances, he says.

"If I was good enough to do it while he was working, why am I not good enough now?" asked one irritated wife.

Schools of thought on solutions run in two directions for this problem. One wife said, "Taking care of bills was a headache I didn't enjoy. Hand them over and find something wonderful to do with the spare time you now have."

Another remarked, "I enjoy keeping accounts, but if handling the money makes him feel as if he's still captain of our budget ship, I'm not going to rock the boat."

Several wives went along with this last decision, but

another woman said, "I did let him take the books over, and within three months he'd gotten us overdrawn twice and forgotten to pay an electric bill. On the fourth month, he handed the books back and went fishing. Suited me just fine."

All women queried said they definitely preferred to have a little money that didn't have to be accounted for, and they most certainly wanted to be in on any big expenditures.

"We're in this retirement together, and I don't feel that just because he is the man of the family, he is necessarily the expert in purchasing, certainly not the household appliances I will be using. I want to be right there to put in my two cents."

In the area of handling family finances, there is no pat answer. It's whatever works for you two. Remember that even if you were never employed outside your home for the forty years you've been married, you worked for whatever money you two have as much as he did. You are entitled to a say in how it is dispensed.

28

HE'S A SPOILED BRAT, AND I MADE HIM THAT WAY

They were young when they married. He worked hard to support the family and she worked hard to support him—so hard she never gave him the opportunity to grow as a husband and a human being.

When he arrived home after work, he sank into his chair, hand extended for a drink. After supper he returned to his chair or went off to a friend's house to spend the evening working on a jolly project. On weekends he went golfing, hunting, or fishing or engaged in other activities with his friends. After a hard week's work, he needed some relaxation time, he told his wife, Gloria. No church with the children for him either; since his job was indoors, he needed the weekends for outside recreation.

She juggled the family books to keep him in sporting equipment. Different cars were his passion and she never knew what it was to have a title to an auto—just payment books. On the few occasions when they went out with their children, he didn't carry packages or push baby buggies.

Everyone in his family had a temper, so how could he be otherwise? Temper tantrums directed at the wife working so hard to please him were an everyday occurrence and always, somehow, he managed to make her feel she had caused them.

He was always more tired than she was, sicker than she was, and certainly more intelligent than she was, and always someone else needed his company more than she did.

Lest you think I made up this martyred woman out of whole cloth, let me assure you that she did exist. I should know. I'm that woman. I finally grew up at 52, walked out of the house and the marriage, had a fine career and wound up marrying a wonderful man.

But not all women walk out of a marriage to a spoiled brat. For reasons of their own, they stay right with the lout until death do them part, and that includes retirement, too.

Marriage will not necessarily change a spoiled brat into an unselfish man. The bad habits acquired as a child—perhaps strengthened by overly doting parents—may continue on through the years. While interviewing I encountered one woman so worried about her husband's possible retirement that she's already in therapy. "I could live with it while we were both working, but if we're together all the time, I just don't know what is going to happen," she said.

But what if you aren't in therapy, you don't want to walk out on the marriage, and you love your husband enough to try to work out a retirement plan?

It's not going to be easy after years of giving in. Are you ready to practice a mature version of Tough Love? This theory of getting tough and making reasonable behavioral demands while showing the person you love him or her was developed for juveniles, but there is no reason it shouldn't apply to a marriage. It is time to stand up *to* your husband and *for* yourself. This means telling your husband that while you still love him and want to stay married to him, you will no longer be his personal handmaiden and whipping girl. You two are going to have to sit down and talk about changes that need to be made in your relationship.

When you make these statements, you may get one of the following reactions.

—He will look at you before blowing up and disappearing to wherever he pleases and coming home whenever he chooses.

—He will look at you with cold contempt and retire to the den, remote control in hand. He'll spend the time in there sulking and emerge only when it's mealtime.

—He will look at you and say, "What do you mean? I don't know what you're talking about."

If he leaves the house, wait until the next day and give him the same speech. When you two do talk, outline your wishes carefully without the fatal phrase "You always . . ." cropping up. Express your wants as concisely and as lovingly as possible. Repeat your requests and solutions as often as it takes. And from then on, live your life as you want to. Don't be afraid to let some of your house duties fall by the wayside. Take care of yourself, be nice to yourself, and always remember, you're entitled to a life of your own.

If he retires to the den, only to emerge for dinner, he will be surprised to find you calmly eating your own dinner. Don't bring up the subject during the meal, but as soon as is feasible, ask him to discuss with you the changes that should be made. Keep making that request until you've got him listening. State your case, listen to his and try to arrive at a reasonable settlement.

If he looks at you and says, "What do you mean? I don't know what you're talking about," then count yourself lucky. You've got a dialogue started, and that's the first step. Bring out your list and quietly, but firmly, make your play.

If you're one of the lucky ladies who haven't created a monster of a spoiled brat, you may be exclaiming, "There really can't be husbands like this." But, you're wrong. Mates like this do exist, and at the time of retirement they may make their wives even more miserable because their lives lack focus and there's only one person to blame. Who? You've already guessed that, haven't you?

If you are a wife with a spoiled brat of a husband, take heart. The end of his work life may be a new beginning of your marriage if you're strong enough and care enough to make the changes.

29

DIVISION OF LABOR: DON'T BE A DRONE WHILE HE HAS ALL THE FUN

One of the reasons this book on living with retired husbands came into being was a conversation overheard on the golf course.

A man, just having received an invitation to play golf from his pal, replied, "I can't on Monday. That's my day to vacuum."

Well, I thought, some wife enjoys a satisfactory arrangement with her husband on the division of labor in retirement. I began to wonder if this consideration was a given in other marriages where the husband is retired.

It most definitely is not, I found on researching this book.

One wife reported that when she and her husband retired at the same time, gave up the family home, and moved into an adult living community with compact-size homes, her husband said, "Now that we're retired, I don't think we need a housekeeper anymore. We can do the work ourselves."

The wife wholeheartedly agreed. The husband said, "Well, that's settled," and went about his own activities. In the days that followed, he developed a great routine while she, angry and resentful, stayed at home with the housework.

A still-working wife told her story: "I'd come home after a hard day's work and find him lying on the couch, book in hand. 'What have you done today?' I'd ask, and he'd reply. 'Nothing. Don't you remember? I'm retired.' "

This went on for about three weeks until she, tired to the bone and not one to hold things in, exploded: "You may have retired from employment, John, but you haven't retired from marriage, so start giving me a hand."

It was a tough fight at first because he was of the old school, a man who believed that housework was woman's work.

The retired wife sulked, fretted and became sour. The working wife nagged, cried and shouted. A year later they both admit that their methods were not the ones they would advocate now for getting an absent or prone husband into a partnership.

A different problem occurred in the "The Case of the Unequal Incomes." This happened to a couple who had been wed only three years when both retired. The woman, who had married a man with more income, became incensed when he agreed to the yard work as one of his chores, then promptly hired a professional service to do the job and went off to pursue his hobbies. His reply was, "Well, it's done, isn't it?"

She retaliated by hiring a cleaning service to come in and clean the bathrooms once a week. Since her retirement income was far less than his, she handed him the bill: "If you can pay to have your chores done, you can pay for mine, too."

He was upset at her attitude, and she really didn't feel good about the way she had handled the problem. After a little time elapsed and they became less emotional, they discussed the problem. The professionals have been dismissed and he now does the lawn while she cleans the bathrooms. Their marriage is stronger than ever because it has become a real partnership, not a "money means power" struggle.

Here is some advice from wives and husbands who have solved the division of labor problem:

- Make an appointment with your husband about a discussion on chores. Don't land on him with unexpected demands. Few husbands—or wives either, for that matter—take well such shocks, which will be perceived as commands. When you do sit down for a discussion, you may get one of several reactions. He may say "sure" to your proposals, then procrastinate. He may do his share of the chores eventually, but in his own time when you are probably pulling your hair out from frustration.

- Be fair about your requests. If you are still working, you have the right to ask for more than a wife who is at home all day. If you're both retired, the division should be equal.

- When working out a division of labor schedule, don't forget, as one man complained in Key 35, the tasks a wife takes for granted. Cleaning out the garage, taking out garbage and other such jobs are work. As one man puts it, "Taking a load of cuttings and rubbish to the dump is not my idea of a fun job. It is a major chore. I wish my wife would see it that way."

- Before making the list, discuss what tasks you each like or really hate. If there is one task you both abhor (cleaning the shower stall heads the personal hate list for both my husband and me), then take turns doing the chore.

- Many wives consider cooking their duty and theirs alone. If a husband wants to try out his culinary skill, grit your teeth and let him go to it. Other husbands want no part of cooking. One retired state police officer told his wife, "I'm never going to want to cook, but if you prepare the meals, I'll do the cleanup." Lucky wife that she is, she immediately agreed.

Although it is not the happiest of thoughts, there may come a time when one spouse becomes incapacitated and the other must take on the chores—all of them. So no matter how you and your mate divvy up the labor, there should be a period of interchange of duties so that each partner knows all there is to know about operating a house and a car.

One wife, who had never driven the car, took herself off to driving school and, for her husband's retirement gift, showed him her driver's license. Having been worried about being his wife's only means of transportation, this retired husband was ecstatic at his gift.

Working out an equitable division of labor list is an extremely important part of retirement, but don't let it be so inflexible that you're not willing to take on an extra task if your mate has something special on tap.

30

OTHER WOMEN: DON'T GET COMPLACENT

"I should have known something was wrong when my husband got braces on his teeth at age 61," said Sally, a trim blonde of 60. "But I didn't. I was a complacent wife of 41 years, and to have Theo chasing women was the last thing I'd accuse him of. However, when he retired at 62, he came in one morning and said, 'I'm celebrating an early retirement with an overdue divorce.' "

The couple's marriage had been in trouble for many years. A retired military man with a dominant personality and a feisty Italian lady with equally strong ideas do make for an inflammable marriage. However, the two had stayed married, despite roof-raising quarrels, and they'd raised three daughters. Sally had always assumed they'd finish their years together.

Kitty's husband walked out on the deck one day and said, "I'm leaving."

She replied, "Will you pick up some bread when you're out?"

He answered, "I mean I'm leaving for good." And he was gone after 38 years of marriage.

Chances are you're never going to be in this situation, but it is not unheard of for men of retirement age to find pleasure in other women's company, said a personal counselor. Other women can be some men's way of combating age and mortality, because they believe that a new woman means added life—especially if the woman is younger.

A man who succumbed to the advances of a younger

woman confided, "An older man just doesn't have a chance when a young woman goes after him. He may know in his heart that it's wrong and won't last, but he's almost powerless to resist."

Sally and Kitty both say now that there were clues that should have tipped them off long before their husbands made the big announcement, and from their experience, offer these tips:

- Their first commandment: Don't be complacent. You probably don't realize how attractive your husband is to other women, especially women who don't have men of their own, or women who are attracted by an older man's financial status.
- Watch for changes in routine. If your husband has a daily routine and begins varying it, he may just be bored and wanting a change of pace. But the change of pace might be to see a new woman. Kitty's husband began taking a walk to get cigarettes even though he had cigarettes in the house. "It didn't register that he might have to walk by the house of my best friend, a widow, to get to the convenience store."
- If one of your single friends begins calling your husband to help her with household problems, it might not be a bad idea to go right along to help, too, advised Kitty. In addition to the "cigarette strolls," her friend often called for Kitty's husband to "help her with the VCR, or start the lawnmower, or perform some other service." Kitty's husband is now married to the ex-best friend and living right down the street with her.
- If he's on the phone and hangs up when you enter the room or begins talking about generic subjects in loud tones, it may be your birthday surprise. Then again there may be another surprise on the way.
- Grooming habits. Both Kitty and Sally said that when their husbands became interested in other women, there was a new attention paid to personal grooming.

Kitty's husband shaved off his long-cherished beard which was showing streaks of gray. Extra aftershave splashed on before a trip to have the car lubricated was a giveaway, said Sally, who added that vanity was not the norm for her husband until he upgraded his appearance by getting his teeth straightened.

- Finances. Unless they are wealthy, retired couples are on a fixed income and, therefore, extra expenses are easy to spot, said Kitty, who found unexplained phone calls on their usually routine phone bill. It turned out that the calls had been made to the widow, who was visiting in another city. If you question some calls, check them out with the telephone company. Either your peace of mind will be restored, or your suspicions will be confirmed. If the latter, you'll have to decide how to deal with the situation.
- Name-dropping. Men and women alike have a habit of saying their new beloved's name as often as they can. This is, as one poet said, "as satisfying as caramel on their tongue."

If your husband, like the husbands of Kitty and Sally, does come up with a request for a divorce, here is the women's advice:

- Even if you're devastated, try to be calm. Do not react in any way, especially by weeping and pleading, Sally said. This puts a husband in a position of power. Try to sit calmly and listen to what he is saying. Let him wind down, look him in the eye, shake your head as if puzzled, and walk out of the room. This is unnerving to a man who's probably been trying to get up his courage for weeks.
- Do not pry for details. You may hear more than you want to know. If you take him back, he may have conjured up visual images you'll have to live with for the rest of your life.
- Do not under any circumstances sign papers he may

112

thrust at you. Some rats, as did Sally's rat, say, "There's no use for us to have two attorneys. It will cost too much. We'll use my attorney." Don't fall for that one. It's the rest-of-your-life income that's at stake here. Reply calmly, "No, I have my own attorney. He'll look over the papers."

- If it is at all possible, leave the house—the longer period of time the better—after he's dropped the bombshell. Sally suggested that, after shaking your head as if you're dealing with a demented person, you pack some things, leave the house and go to the home of a sympathetic child or friend. Or even check into a motel. Stay there for several days, a week if you possibly can. While alone, write down your feelings every hour or so. Sally did this and said it helped her put things into perspective. She also added: "My disappearance drove him crazy because he was being ignored and had no resolution in sight. He hated the uncertainty."

- If you want to salvage this marriage, you may want to seek professional counseling. If it's impossible to get him there—and retirement age men often look upon counseling as a weakness—then go by yourself. Be open with your counselor and be willing to acknowledge that perhaps you helped drive away your mate. Husbands are not purses to be "stolen," but they can be lost through carelessness or apathy.

- If your husband comes back after his fling, as did Sally's, there are things you must do, she said, adding that it doesn't pay to subject him to recriminations about his straying or to punish him by withholding sex. Don't hold back sex, she cautioned, although you may have to grit your teeth for a while. "If you take him back because you really want him back, make it worth his trip home," she advised.

31

SEX IN THE AFTERNOON? WHY NOT?

One of the most important aspects of marriage after retirement is your sex life.

Billie, a charming woman of 63, says frankly, "If I am keeping him happy in bed, retired life is a lot easier. And I'm not complaining, I like it!"

If your partner is like most men, your retired-life sex will take one of two directions:

—He'll want sex more often, and at times you're not going to believe.

—He'll shy away from intimate encounters. This is not healthy for either of you, and certainly not healthy for a marriage. You have a problem here that needs to be resolved through frank discussion or counseling.

Let's talk about the husbands who look upon retirement as one gigantic sex binge. Count yourself lucky if your husband falls into this category, because sex, especially with older men, is a means of self-proof as much as it is pleasure. If your husband is creating so much sexual energy, he is proclaiming (1) I am alive, (2) I can still perform the sex act, and (3) I can still please a woman.

A man's sex drive, or lack thereof, is a very fragile portion of his ego. If it diminishes, a man's will to live can often go right along with it; so it is up to you to help keep this physical part of your marriage alive and functioning. When you're of retirement age, the hot excitement of your youth may have simmered down to a warm feeling of love and affection, but this shouldn't mean that the fun and games have ended.

How can a loving wife jump-start a sputtering sex life?

- Be spontaneous. He'll enjoy the change and begin to look forward to seeing what you've got in store for him. Madge invited Mort to "let's make up in bed" after the couple had had a quarrel. He was fascinated. But you don't have to quarrel to end up in bed in the middle of the afternoon. That's the joy of life after retirement—do whatever you want whenever you want.

- Older men often have a stronger sex drive in the morning—something to do with testosterone buildup. So if he's been acting cool lately, don't leap out of bed to do your exercises. Roll over and cuddle with him.

- Have you taken a good look at your lingerie lately? Are you by any chance wearing grannie gowns? They may be cute for teen-agers, but real grannies look doubly dowdy in the sack garments. Provocative lingerie in all sizes is available now. And don't wait until after the eleven o'clock news to appear in your new concoction. What's wrong with changing into "something more comfortable" just after supper?

- Don't faint if I suggest X-rated movies just for the two of you. They're inspiring! Tip from one who knows: Don't rent them at your favorite video store where you're known. The tipster, a retired school-teacher, was greeted by the clerk with a "Hi, Mrs. X. Remember me? I was in your history class." She paled, then beat a hasty retreat to put back the X-rater and reappear with *The Sound of Music*. No— best to do your rentals where you're not known.

- If your husband makes some interesting suggestions that are foreign to his usual tastes, go along with them—unless it involves pains or chains, of course.

- Don't be afraid to be a little silly. Remember all those

115

crazy little buzzwords you and your husband used when you were newlyweds? Cozy up and trot them out. He'll love it that you remember.

- If things don't quite work out, he may feel awful. That's your cue to be extra loving and affectionate. There's always tomorrow—or 30 minutes from now if he's interested.

Now, about the husband who has turned his back on sex: It could be that he's afraid he can't perform, or it could be that he's not feeling well. If it's the former, try some of the suggestions just listed. If his lack of drive continues, get him to a doctor with whom he feels comfortable enough to confide his problem.

Let's talk about you now. If you're a wife whose husband is no longer interested, and you say, "Well, thank goodness that's over," I believe you'll be missing some of retired life's finest moments. If you want to change, then go back to the beginning of this key and pay attention to the tips. They can work as well for you as they do for him.

Final tip: Keep your sense of humor about sex. It's not a do-or-die situation unless you make it so.

32

ROUTINES: LIFESAVERS OR RUTS?

One of the delights of retirement is freedom from the daily work grind. "In this life, there are no Monday mornings," said one joyous retiree.

But if you don't have to get up to go to work, what do you have to get up for? Of course, you can sleep away the day, as you so often dreamed about while getting dressed for work, but is that what you really want? If you do, maybe this section is not for you.

It's been drilled into most of us that life without a purpose is no life at all. Your husband has been retired a week and is beginning to be a tad touchy. You are feeling a little blah yourself. What's missing here?

A routine. But we don't want a routine, you're saying. Isn't that the point of retirement, getting out of the rut of a routine?

Well, sure, but that doesn't mean you can't replace grueling routines with pleasant routines; and it may fall to you, the wife, to imaginatively devise such routines for a retired husband who can't figure out what to do next.

Sure, it's normal to assume that he's going to get up in the morning. (But if he doesn't, you may want to refer to Key 49 about danger signals.) OK, he's up; what are you going to do next? If you're like most couples, you're going to have breakfast and read the paper. So you did that before you went to work? Nothing new about this routine.

What's different? Perhaps it's the time you get up. One man rose every morning at six, left the house

117

promptly at 6:44 A.M., and went downtown. No, that's not a typo—he actually left the house at 6:44, no earlier, no later, to have coffee with his friends. Then he headed off to his business.

After the couple moved away from the small town and into the city, he kept rising at six o'clock but there was no place to go. Gradually, with a little cuddling and coaxing from his wife, he began sleeping until 7:30 A.M.

His wife is jubilant. With this later sleep time, she actually has good company with her at night, clear up through the eleven o'clock news—no recumbent figure in the reclining chair, snoring his way through prime-time TV.

She'd helped him change his routine without his really being aware of what he was doing.

Routines in retirement can be as loose or as structured as a couple want to make them. So, what are some healthy and fulfilling routines you can ease into after a life of work? This list was compiled from happy wives of retired husbands:

• Donate one day a week to helping others, more days if you're so inclined. One couple deliver Meals on Wheels to shut-ins every Tuesday and Thursday. They each take their own car, drive to the church where the meals are dispensed and go on their individual rounds. Over dinner that night, they discuss their deliveries. Every two weeks or so, they switch rounds so that each can visit the people the other spouse has visited. "Tuesdays and Thursdays have special meaning for us. Really a reason to get up and get going," said the wife.

• Instead of collapsing on the couch and filling the morning with TV, one wife suggested they start walking. They began with a short stroll around their neighborhood and have now worked up to five miles a day. A stop for tea and muffins along the way provides a treat on their healthful trek.

- Daytime TV? Eeeek! No need to shun daytime TV completely, said one woman. She and her husband prefer to take their walk after lunch. They get up in the morning and have their coffee watching "Good Morning, America" or CNN for at least 45 minutes. "We feel we have a window view of the world this way, and whatever we see makes for conversation during our walks."

- One duo like to drive, so one day a week is set aside for a little trip around the countryside. They have lunch out, sometimes at a charming country inn, other times at fast-food chains. "I'm a lucky woman. I found out that Harve has patience for my 'junking' hobby, so we stop at garage sales and secondhand stores. He likes old books on sports and I like to look at everything. Our once-a-week jaunt gives us something to look forward to."

- A day for gardening is the routine of one retired couple. The "day" may differ from one week to the next, depending on weather, but setting one day aside for lawn and flowerbed duties is not a despised routine for this couple. They enjoy being out in the fresh air and are now experimenting with seedlings and talking about setting up a tiny greenhouse.

- Sunday brunch? Agnes and Walt, who live on a small but steady income, enjoy a dining-out treat every Sunday morning. Sometimes their brunch will be at McDonald's for a Sausage McMuffin, sometimes at fancier places for eggs benedict. Recently, they went to a Mexican restaurant and had their first taste of huevos rancheros, a spicy egg dish. "Breakfast or brunch is the cheapest meal to eat out," said Agnes,

119

who is delighted. "Sometimes we'll go before church, sometimes after. Whatever, it makes Sunday a special treat."

Retirement need not mean a change of routines, rather an exchange of routines, and the most joyous thing about retirement routines is that they can merrily be broken any time you like.

33

ESCAPE ROUTES: EVERY WIFE NEEDS THEM

Although being a wife and mother is an important part of a woman's life, she should also remember her needs as an individual. Every wife, whether she works outside the home or is a full-time homemaker, needs to devise an escape route to use when life gets too stressful. When her inner voice warns, "Enough, lady," she should head toward her own particular bolt hole, wherever it may be.

One of the first keys to living with a retired husband is learning to live with and take care of yourself in this retirement situation. A woman can be overwhelmed by the magnitude of this new and sometimes frightening experience. Don't allow your household to revolve around the wants of the retiree, and certainly don't allow yourself to be maneuvered into becoming a personal bond servant, especially if you've been out working all day. You still need time for yourself. And don't back down when you state your needs and your husband reminds you that your duty lies in being a wife.

Remember, he is no doubt just as overwhelmed as you and is also reaching out for a new identity, but don't let this fact intimidate you. You are you, and retirement should herald the start of your own personal best years. Be nice to yourself. These are the years in which you can indulge yourself in whatever strikes your fancy.

So what does strike your fancy? What is it that interests you?

Naomi found rest and relaxation in painting. The

interest had been kindled in high school and fueled by two years in college, where she majored in art. When Josh returned from the service and made his play for her, Naomi threw college to the winds, got married, had two children and spent the majority of her life taking care of Josh and the kids. Then they retired to a coastal community condo.

Now that there were free hours for her she began taking classes in watercolors, which she found more challenging than oils. She also joined a local art guild, whose members hang exhibits and staff the gallery. Naomi has plenty of time to love and cherish her husband, as well as her family, which she sees two or three times a month, but her art time is her time, and she is ecstatic about her perfect life.

If you have no particular escape route planned, here are some ways to get started:

- First decide what it is that interests you most—none of that "I should do something that will benefit my family" stuff—this is for you and you alone. If it's something as luxuriously useless as conversational French, when you're sure you won't be going to France, take it anyway. You'll have fun, meet interesting people, and be able to dazzle your friends by reading and translating the menu at French restaurants.
- Still not sure? Get a list of classes from your local schools and community college. There are scads of classes available, ranging from archaeology to zoology. You're sure to find something that piques your interest.
- Interest piqued? Now get going. Don't put it off by saying, "Well, first I'll clean out those kitchen cupboards and catch up with my ironing." Find your escape route and just take off!
- Too timid to go alone? Call a friend. She may be at

loose ends too, and grateful for your call. Half the fun of an escape route is being able to talk about it or enjoy it with friends.

Here are some specific suggestions from women who've discovered their own particular joy:

• Janie took classes in traditional and Japanese flower arranging through the public school's adult education program. Now she's in great demand for her talents and has been asked to judge arrangements at the state fair.

• Gena answered an ad for women wanted to pass out products at a large supermarket. A gregarious soul with a super-quiet husband, Gena now spends four or five days a month passing out ice cream, tiny sausages, or pizza rounds for whatever manufacturer needs her. She's making a little money and loves talking to the passersby.

• Gloria finds escape in British mysteries both in print and on TV. It doesn't get her out of the house, but the highly stylized structure of the English mystery takes her right out of her own world and into another.

• Tap dancing? Well, why not? Donna, a firm believer in exercise who walks five miles a day with her husband, needed some fun on her own. She signed up at the senior center and taps her heart out once a week. No plans for show biz, she says; just fun and a great way to stay trim.

• History was always Anne's passion, so she signed up as a guide through pioneer homes at her city's historic complex. "I love to show people, especially children, how their ancestors lived, but I think I even enjoy it more when everyone is gone and I can sit quietly in one of the restored rooms and breathe in the past. I am so moved I may start writing a novel!

• Linda began making teddy bears for her own children, then her grandchildren. Now that she and her husband are retired, she turns out teddies by the score. Once a year she hauls her bears—nattily attired in a variety of costumes—to a holiday show and brings home a nice bit of cash.

Whatever your passion, indulge it. Don't ever feel guilty about your desire to please yourself. You can be totally committed to husband and marriage and still allot some time for you.

Listen to the advice of a family counselor who says: "In my counseling work, I've found that though husbands may complain about the time spent away from them, they have a lot of respect for a wife who is not afraid to take the time to be herself."

34

POWER PLAYS: KEEPING ONE STEP AHEAD OF HIM ALL THE WAY

I doubt there's a wife who hasn't been a victim of husbandly power play. Even the most wonderful husbands have their little ways of keeping us in line and performing as they think we should.

A discussion group of 20 wives of retired husbands examined the "power play" strategies used by their husbands in certain situations, and offered some suggestions for dealing with them.

The following are the most common ploys, the wives reported. Recognize any of them?

- "You won't need the car today, will you? I'm going to get the oil changed." Sylvia said her husband uses this one when he knows she has plans with a friend or if he thinks she has and he feels her place is at home. "He always uses it when he has some shirts that need ironing," she reported.

- "Don't plan anything for Sunday. The Pebble Beach Pro-Am tournament is on and I don't want to miss it." This, or any variation thereof, is generally voiced by Ralph, said his wife, Winnie, "if he has a clue that something not quite to his liking is in the works."

- "Have a good time with Rhonda, but don't forget to be back by 5:00 P.M." Why? "George tells me he doesn't want me out in the rush hour traffic," said wife Rose, "but I think it's his little power play to ensure that his supper is going to be on time."

- Here is one of the most common ploys reported by

wives at the interview. You're at a meeting or having coffee at a friend's house. Ring! It's your husband. "Now what time did you say you were coming home? I need the car." He may indeed have forgotten, but wives interviewed maintain that he knows exactly what time you said you'd be home and this is just his little niggle to command your presence at his convenience.

- "You're 30 minutes later than you said you would be. I was worried about you." Not really. "He just wants me where he wants me when he wants me," is a typical retired-wife power-play complaint.

Are these women too critical of a loving and caring man? If you think so, either your marriage was made in heaven or you may be entirely too naive to protect yourself from husbandly power plays—like my co-worker Grace in Key 23. She was manipulated into feeling guilty by a master of the game and never tumbled to that fact.

Marriage is a loving partnership and as in any other partnership, power shifts from person to person from day to day.

In order not to let the power shift away from you too often, you must sometimes gently shake up your mate by changing your pattern of replies and your attitude toward his maneuvers.

For example, if he books the car ahead without asking you and you don't have plans of your own, smile graciously and say, "That's fine with me, darling." But if you do have plans, smile just as graciously and say, "I really would like the car that day. Could you make it another time? I'll call and reschedule for you if you like."

To the "Don't plan anything for Sunday" ploy, you may answer: "Oh, that's fine. I'll just go over to my friend Betty's house, or to our son Bill's, or to the mall."

He's hoist on his own petard here. He's home alone, and he's done it to himself.

For the rush-hour-traffic fret, don't commit. Smile and say, "I'll do my best, but I can't promise anything. That traffic, you know." There's little he can say.

If he bugs you with the "I can't remember when you said you were coming home" routine, just sweetly answer: "I didn't really say, but I'll be home as soon as we're finished here." No promises, just a polite response that tells him, "I love you, but don't push me."

And for the "later than you said" routine, just say, "Well, I tried," and let it go at that.

Husbands after retirement, as much as we love them, still play the "this is your captain speaking" game. You don't have to put up with this unless you want to. A smile, a kiss, and a kind but firm reply can scuttle any "captain" routine and bring your husband back into the partnership.

35

LITTLE THINGS MEAN A LOT: HOW TO LIVE WITH THEM

We've talked about the resentment you may feel when you wake up the morning after your husband's retirement and realize that your domestic domain is not entirely yours anymore. And just what is he feeling and what are his resentments against you?

Four wives and four retired husbands air their areas of discontent and the ways they have worked to resolve the differences.

From the wives:

—"My doing household chores is a given. His doing chores is a gallant act. Why is this when he is no longer employed outside the home?"

The speaker is a witty woman in her mid-sixties. She advises bringing to mind fairly often, without putting him down, that he no longer has eight hours of work to do and that home chores are now "our chores," not "your chores unless I choose to do them," as some men retort when asked to perform what they consider a woman's task.

—To the "Why must I always be the one to take out the garbage?" question, this wife answers, "Because I am always the one to cook the meals. Any time you'd like to switch duties, I'm open to change!"

—Disposition of the morning mail bugs Betty. "I used to get the mail, pore through it and enjoy it all, even the junk mail. Now that he's home, the mail is under his control. I swear the older he gets, the more important the morning mail becomes. It's as if he's expecting an invitation from Buckingham Palace. Our mail has become his mail. He hasn't quite gotten to the point of opening any mail addressed to me, but I think it's close. And if I don't move quickly, he decides the disposition of what he considers junk mail. He'll toss out a catalog if it doesn't appeal to him, and I love catalogs!"

How can this problem be solved? Betty answers, "Make a fuss! Sometimes there's no other way. I nag. Where is the mail? Is this all there was? I look in the trash and if I produce something I consider worthwhile, I take it into the house, confront him with it and ask why he threw it away. I remind him that his idea of junk mail might be just what I've been waiting for."

—"He hogs the whole newspaper" was the complaint of many wives. "I have my morning chores, and I like to get them done after I read the paper. Now that he's home, he reads one section while holding onto the rest. I have to wait until he portions it out, section by section. It drives me mad," said Ruby.

She advises getting up a little earlier and grabbing the paper first. "Let me tell you, he doesn't like having his sections doled out to him. I made my point."

—"My husband sets the chores schedule," said one wife. "He'll say, 'I'll help you make the bed if you do it right now.' No matter if I am in the middle of washing my hair. If he has an errand to do, it takes precedence over whatever I've asked him to do. Any suggestion I make takes second priority."

A wife is pretty well caught on this one. If he offers help on an "it must be done now" basis, she has to decide whether to accept the help on his terms or do the job alone. She might try, "Just a minute, while I finish what I'm doing." A sensible man will wait for this. She could put up a schedule of when chores are to be done, but this is pretty structured, and you don't want to run your house like a military establishment. This may be a grin-and-bear-it situation.

From the husbands:

—"I think her friends and her organizations take priority over me. She'll go out of her way to help her friends when they ask, but when I ask for something I wait for days for her to get around to doing it."

Ladies, this was a complaint from several men, so think it over. You may have to reprioritize your activities and perhaps drop some of your social and club duties. After all, he is Numero Uno in your life, isn't he?

—"She makes social engagements without consulting me" was also a common complaint. Wives should always give their husbands the courtesy of having a say about their social life. Think how unhappy you would be if he excluded you from social decisions. Accepting or declining invitations is definitely something you should do together.

When acquaintances put you on the spot with an invitation, answer them with a "That sounds lovely. I'll talk it over with Fred to see what he has planned for that evening." It's only polite. However, if your fellow isn't very communicative about what he wants or does not want to do, keep after him. Sit there and wait for an answer before commiting you both to an engagement.

—"She wants to divide the chores now that I'm retired, but when it comes to adding up the workload, she forgets or takes it for granted about my cleaning the garage, raking the leaves, mowing the grass, taking the car to be serviced. That's not fair," said one disgruntled husband.

Being fair is very much a part of married life, retired or otherwise. Don't be afraid to ask for help with the house, but do take a good look at the husbandly duties you may be taking for granted.

—"She gets so defensive or goes on the offensive when I ask a simple question beginning with how, what, or when." Several husbands mentioned this problem, which corresponds with complaints voiced by wives. Husbands have a point here, because some wives think they are being put on the spot when husbands ask for information. Before you retreat or blow up, try to evaluate why your husband is asking the question. He may not mean to be accusatory at all; maybe he's curious or just making conversation.

In a marriage, little things can build up into big things when one or the other partner silently seethes rather than bringing the problem to the surface. Unexpressed resentment over slights or neglects can lead to an accumulation and eventual explosion of anger.

Using a give-and-take discussion, many of these problems can be quickly and easily solved by opening up the channels of communication mentioned in Key 6. Remember, mind reading is not part of the marriage contract. Unless we tell our mates what we feel and think, they cannot be expected to know what's in our hearts and minds.

36

THE SUPERMARKET RHUBARB

While I was researching this book, I interviewed scores of wives who had advice and solutions for living with a retired husband. After several months of intense questioning and listening, I discovered one retired-husband habit that sends wives into emotional binges ranging from silent seething to out-and-out temper tantrums.

Simply put, it is supermarket shopping. If you haven't tried serious grocery shopping with your husband, you'll wonder why I'm devoting an entire section to what appears to you as an inconsequential problem. If shopping à deux is no problem to you and your mate, count yourself lucky. But mention supermarket shopping to many women with full-time husbands and you'll probably get an earful.

Most wives do the weekly shopping for groceries and cleaning supplies. Preretirement husbands generally just pick up an item or two on their way home from work. Most women have strong feelings about supermarket shopping. Some hate to shop, but they do it; it is, they feel, their job. For some, it is almost a social outing, because you're likely to find friends in the aisles. Others love grocery shopping because it is an opportunity to spend money without feeling guilty. Some live for the adrenalin spurt that comes when you bring the total in at less than you planned. To other wives, coupon clipping is a religion, and they wouldn't miss their chance at the big checkout payoff.

Whatever the feelings, wives and husbands shopping

together can sometimes result in full-blown supermarket rhubarbs, because some retired men feel it is their duty to see where all the money is going.

Firsthand and without exaggeration, I observed the following scenario: This retired couple were in the produce department. As she walked through shopping, he followed behind pushing the cart. Each time she placed a bag of fruit or vegetables into the cart, the husband, without fail, examined it as if it were being offered for display at the state fair.

She bought apples. He discarded three of her choices. She bought Roma tomatoes. He pooh-poohed the whole batch and put them back, reaching for the salad tomatoes, which were 30 cents a pound less. No matter that they were a sickly pink and were bound to be tasteless. He was certain he'd made the better bargain selection.

I could see her quietly fuming. When he began to rifle through the bag of fresh mushrooms she'd chosen, she blew.

"You think you know so much! Here's the list! You do the shopping!" and away she stomped, presumably out to the car to (rightfully, to my mind) sulk.

I wondered what that couple's drive home was like. Would they speak? Probably not. Had he gotten through the rest of the list and known what he was looking for? Would he know that "fab sftn" was her shorthand for fabric softener? Eventually they had to make up, but would the problem happen again? Probably.

There's no way we can know how this wife settled the problem of the Hovering Husband in the supermarket, but the wives I interviewed offered this advice:
• If he is determined to go with you, make two lists: one for him and one for you. When you enter the market, hand him his list and each get a cart; then

determine how long it's going to take (synchronize your watches) and where you will meet. One woman reported losing a husband for 45 minutes in a supermarket. He was at the magazine rack, list unfilled, reading electronics magazines.

- Whenever possible, let him do *all* the shopping. Hand him a carefully printed list and send him to the store. Wives agreed, although none could answer just why, that men take anywhere from 30 minutes to an hour longer than they did buying the same items.

- One wife reported that her husband carefully cut coupons out of the newspapers; then left them to expire in a counter canister. Then when she brought home an item for which he'd cut a coupon, he demanded to know why she hadn't taken the coupon. Therefore, when they went shopping, she craftily included on his list, which she had handed him at home, the items for which she knew he had cut coupons. If he remembered the coupons, wonderful; if he had forgotten them or they were expired, then let it be on his head.

- If you are a wife who really doesn't give a rip about shopping, give him a list and let him go. It'll do him good to see how much things cost anyway, and just wait until he gets behind someone who has twenty dollars' worth of coupons *and* can't find his checkbook. Hah! While he's gone, pick up your favorite book or a just-arrived magazine, fix yourself a cup of tea, sit back and enjoy. You'll have several hours of delightfully free time.

37

YOU LOVE HIM, BUT YOU DON'T LIKE HIM?

He's home. You're home. You're together full-time for the first time in your entire married life, and you've just discovered a very distressing fact. You love this man, but you don't really like him.

Full-time marriage has a way of accentuating faults that were easy—more or less—to ignore when you weren't together all of the time. Now that you two are in too-close tandem, you're getting more and more irritable.

The first thing you must do is to define exactly what it is that's bothering you. Maybe it's a surface irritation that a bit of one-on-one communication, with a little humor thrown in, can alleviate. Maybe it's as much you as it is him. You're not used to sharing your life and you're feeling a bit trapped.

So what is it that's bugging you?

—"I never knew he had such a bad mouth," one woman reported. "Every other word that comes out is a four-letter word or even worse. Maybe he knew enough to tone it down when we were raising the children, but he called me a dumb bitch yesterday and I was ready to walk out until he apologized. Now I'm just waiting for the next time. If he did it once, he can do it again."

—His temper is impossible. "I knew he had a bad temper when I married him, but when he'd come home tired at night and blow up, I thought it was because he'd had a bad day. Now he's home and rested and it's still the same," said Georgia. "His entire family had bad tempers. His grandmother died of a stroke while screaming at a neighbor about his hose being on her property. My husband says it's just his nature and he can't help it. I say a bad temper is an immature emotional luxury I'm not willing to put up with. I'm not sure I can live with this full-time."

—He's lazy. "When he had to work, he did work hard," said Jeanne. "Now he lies around, or calls for me to wait on him, and when I say, 'Do it yourself,' he replies, 'I'm retired. You're not.' " Just remember, you don't have to be his maid unless you agree to it. If you don't like his demands, don't put up with them. Ignore the requests, let his dirty laundry pile up, and sit down and read a magazine when it's time to fix supper. Two can play at this game. When you feel the time is right, tell him what you're doing and why you're doing it. This may shock him into the reality of retirement.

—He's stubborn to a fault. "Once he's made up his mind, that's the way it's going to be, whatever it is. There is no compromise. He states the way it's going to be and clams up," said one wife on the verge of a frustrated crying jag.

It's up to you to decide how much stubbornness is too much. You can initiate a discussion to outline the problem. If this fails, one wife advised listening quietly to his engraved-in-stone pronouncements, evaluating them and then following your own wishes as much as possible.

—"I'm still working, he's not, but he still won't do anything around the house. He's too busy bowling and shooting pool. He's having a wonderful retired life, playing all the time. I'm too tired to breathe when I finally get to bed; then he wants a good time. I just want to go to sleep."

One working wife in this situation said she hired a cleaning woman twice a week. When he realized how much was coming out of her paycheck, he revised his way of thinking and is now doing things around the house. Not all the work, but enough to where she has the cleaning woman once every two weeks.

—"He's really secretive. He hangs on to the account books like they're military top secrets. I don't know how much money we've got or where he's got it. Ours was a late marriage, so we have his and hers accounts, but I don't like the sneaky way he hides his bank statements the minute they come. I love him, not his money. Why won't he open up to me? Married couples share, don't they?" asks Gladys. If you married later in life, it may be difficult to change him, but you can request those changes.

—"His pals consider our home their home. They're always around drinking beer, watching TV, working on projects in our garage, which is beginning to look like a garbage dump. When I try to talk to him about it, he won't listen. He says, "It's my home. I paid for it. I can do anything I want to in it."

The wife making this complaint tried a variation of Tough Love, that loving but "firm with no-nonsense" technique we talked about in Key 27 to open her husband's eyes. She moved out of the house and in with a single daughter. Eventually, after missing his meals and other comforts, he agreed to send the pals packing. Divorce is now out for this woman, and the situation is improved but not perfect, she said.

—"Should I have this man declared legally dead?" mourned one wife. "He doesn't get excited about anything. He lies like a stone on the couch every evening and rarely speaks. I might as well be alone. I never noticed his lethargy so much while he was working. I just thought he was tired."

This man may be suffering from classic depression, and his wife might do well to seek professional counsel. This is not a situation to be ignored.

—"I never really noticed what a chauvinistic pig my husband is. He is constantly griping about the 'stupid bank teller,' saying that women shouldn't be allowed to handle money, or about the 'dumb girl' at the check-out counter. It just grates on me. If he considers all women dumb, stupid and moronic, what does that make me?"

Although many wives maintain that if you love your husband, it follows that you also like him, just as many women rebut this belief. Most wives continue to love the man they knew, the good times, the sweet and loving gestures of unselfishness, the kindnesses. Others don't even talk of love. They have simply existed with the man they married. It is only in full-time retirement that they find the negative traits almost impossible to deal with. A family counselor said he had encountered one marriage where the wife said, "If we met now, I wouldn't even consider him for a husband."

If the negative traits are too much for the wife, it is up to her to decide what she is going to do about the marriage. If she decides for religious, financial or personal reasons that she will remain in the marriage, then she must find ways to defuse her anger by going out and getting involved in activities that interest her.

A woman who is involved outside the home is less prone to let marital irritations get the best of her. Ways for a wife to "escape" without leaving a marriage are discussed in Key 33. Going back to work, even part-time, is a splendid resolution to this problem. The wife will have the opportunity to meet and talk with new people, and earn her own paycheck, thus ensuring a measure of independence which will help keep her sane.

If a wife decides she simply cannot take living with this man, then she should leave the marriage. This is discussed in Key 48.

38

ORGANIZATIONS: SO YOU SAY YOU'RE NOT A JOINER?

It's a rare person who has maneuvered his or her way through life without joining some sort of group, whether it be as loosely put-together as a neighborhood discussion session or as highly ritualized as the Masons.

If you are a joiner of groups, perfect. You will have your retirement activities partially lined up already. However, if you've never been a joiner, then why not become one now?

What kind of organizations and just how much you are willing to give are prime considerations. Are you in the early stages of retirement and at loose ends? Becoming part of a structured group that has a purpose and offers social interaction is an excellent way to find satisfaction. Everyone needs a reason to get out of bed in the morning, and an organization with meetings to attend, duties to perform, or reports to give, answers this need.

If you are in doubt as to what organization would suit your needs, your local Chamber of Commerce might be a good place to begin. Most people think of the Chamber as an organization geared to active employed business people, but chambers have many members who are retired. Chamber committees may include agriculture/natural resources, local government issues, marketing and communications, social issues, veterans and military affairs, legislative affairs, and education and school issues. Many Chambers also have a "Greeters" group who serve as "ambassadors" for the organization. These tireless folks welcome new businesses and recognize contributions of existing members. Chambers are delighted with retired members as they add great depth of experience to the organization.

Perhaps your local senior center will be just the ticket for you and your spouse. If you've always envisioned a center as a bleak room populated by near-comatose oldsters, it's time to take a look at what America's contemporary senior centers are offering. Centers are abuzz with activities from morning until the doors close at night. One of the most popular events at one such place is the tea dance where seniors dress up in their best and dance to Big Band Era music provided by other members.

A West Coast senior director said her organization has single-interest groups like cardplayers who come in the morning and play all day, as well as group participation activities such as modern and folk dancing, low-impact exercise classes, and games. Hobby groups for those interested in woodworking, ceramics, photography, handbells, and weaving are very popular, the director added.

An important aspect of a Center is the opportunity for seniors to contribute their time to keep the center functioning. With the exception of a few paid staffers, many centers depend on volunteer workers to man the switchboards, act as receptionists, help with class registration, and to chair special events.

In addition to the social and hobby activities, senior centers also offer sessions on financial planning and preparing tax returns and wills, as well as medical advice programs that may include eye exams, hearing clinics and breast cancer clinics. Classes on nutrition and preparing simple well-balanced meals are well attended, said one director, whose center also offers hot lunches at whatever the senior can afford to pay.

She added, "I think senior centers offer the most fun for the least cost, and they are open to everyone no matter the income or education."

If your interests lie somewhere between dedicated community involvement in the Chamber and the "please-yourself" activities of a senior organization, hie yourself down to your local Chamber of Commerce and pick up a list of organizations in your city. You'll be amazed and delighted at the variety of organizations awaiting your participation, each offering new interests and new friends.

39

JOINT PROJECTS: THEY DON'T HAVE TO BE A HASSLE

Sooner or later, you and your loved one will launch upon a joint project. Perhaps, due to the pressures of the workaday world, this will be the first "together" undertaking you've attempted in years, perhaps decades.

Your project may take the form of physical activity, such as a vegetable garden or berry picking in the woods, or a creative venture, such as furniture restoration or painting the house, or even a couch-potato occupation, such as pasting in albums the ten thousand family photos you've been collecting for years.

It is amazing, but put an ordinarily loving husband and wife together on a project and sparks may begin to fly. Many wives reported that even going for a short drive together in the country may turn ugly when the navigator in the passenger seat doesn't read the map the way the captain at the wheel thinks it should be read. I knew a navigator who, pushed beyond her endurance, asked her husband to stop at a service station for a restroom, went right to the phone, called a cab and went home. And they weren't even out of the city in which they live.

True story? You bet. I should know.

However and happily, most husband/wife project problems are not this extreme. The majority just end up with some bickering over who's the boss and why.

I asked a man in his late sixties why men often assume the role of the supervisor in a marital project.

"Well," he said, thinking it over, "somebody has to do it, and I think men are used to taking a leadership role. Once they decide on a project, they plan an attack and take it on, one, two, three. Women usually work around a project rather than tackling it head-on. Seems to take them twice as long as it does a man to get organized, begin and finish."

By the time he finished, I was fuming as, no doubt, most of you are fuming right now. I had an extra right to fume. It was my husband speaking.

Well, I'd asked for a male viewpoint, and I'd gotten one. Now let's hear from the distaff side.

"I don't mind letting him be head honcho if, and this is a big if, the project is in his field of expertise," said a wife of 37 years. "However, if the expertise is mine, then he should be willing to play second banana to my skills."

Sounds logical, doesn't it? But getting a man to take a back seat in a project or even to share the front seat will, if your husband is like many husbands, take some doing.

For *your* project, here's a suggested three-point game plan:

- Decide on the project and its priority in your life. An agreement must be reached on the priority. If it's high on your list, low on his, trouble is brewing right off. This what, when, and how discussion should be serious; no fair sneaking peeks at "As the World Turns" over his shoulder. Neither should he be watching the finals at Wimbledon.
- Project decided upon? Priorities set? It's time to make a list of what's needed to complete the venture and then go to purchase the items. Too often, women are turned into "gofers" sent on their own to the hardware

or garden shop to buy items about which they have little or no knowledge. If husband and wife go together to make the purchases, there is no chance of the old "You forgot..." routine most wives are familiar with.

- Once the purchases and the equipment are assembled, decide upon a work plan. If your husband is supervisor of this particular project, have him explain it to you. If there is any point you're not clear about, ask for a re-explanation; then explain back to him what you heard. Amazing how translations of explanations can take on different versions from one ear to the next.

"Togetherness" projects are common in retired life, so don't hesitate to get involved. But don't become so deadly serious about a project that you forget your sense of humor. If you're not having fun, the project may not be worth doing.

40

LIVING FOR TODAY AND TOMORROW

Sure it's fun to look over old photographs and muse over the mystery of the disappearing waistline or the spindly little boy who grew up to be a six-foot-three corporate executive. But don't make glimpses into the past a way of life for you and your sweetheart.

Retirement usually spells finis to your work life, but it needn't, and you shouldn't let it, spell finis to your life as an active and forward-looking individual.

Remember how as a kid you were always looking forward to the school carnival, Halloween, Christmas, your birthday or a good friend's birthday? There is no reason to abandon those happy "fun in the future" dreams just because a portion of your life is behind you. If you stop to think about it, a portion of your life has always been behind you. Don't toss away old memories—they are precious to the heart—but never forget there is always today, and that is what you should be concentrating on.

To heighten this sense, you must learn to live in the moment at hand. Anthony Trollope, the nineteenth-century British writer who so beautifully chronicled Victorian manners and mores, was said to have a "keen appreciation of the present." The ability to appreciate life as you are living it at this very moment is not always a gift from God. It must be cultivated as devotedly as you cultivate your fragile Sterling Silver roses.

Failing to cultivate happiness, whether for the moment or for the future, can be detrimental to both marriage and mental health. Nathan, a gregarious salesman

146

all his life, developed emphysema—his wife had always told him to stop smoking, but he ignored her—and had to take an early retirement. Subsequently, he went into dreams of past sales, past glories and past good health.

It was a warm and sunny afternoon at the couple's country home. Lannie, his wife, was preparing late Sunday supper because the children and grandchildren were coming over. Nathan kept grousing about one thing or another until finally, in exasperation, his wife said, "Get happy, Nathan!"

He complained, "I have nothing to be happy about."

Lannie reminded him: "The sky is blue, the sun is shining, and our children and grandchildren are healthy and care enough about us to drive over to visit this afternoon."

"But," he said, "I don't know how much longer I have to live."

Certainly with his poor health, this was a valid worry, but no one knows how much longer he or she has to live, and life never should be lived in anticipation of death. Nathan's attitude is a prime example of the old "glass is half full, glass is half empty" adage. Nathan's life was half empty; Lannie's life was half full. Like Trollope, Lannie was not worrying about the future; instead, she was keenly appreciating a Sunday afternoon when all in her world was well.

Helping a spouse rouse from a postretirement depression and begin looking toward the future is part of every good wife's job description, because support of one another is a prime ingredient of a happy marriage.

How best can you establish a "today and tomorrow" attitude in your marriage? Here are some tips:

- A full dance card is wearying, but a calendar dotted with pleasant experiences to come is happiness-making.
- If you two do indulge in a bit of nostalgia over the

old photo album or high school yearbooks, counter the experience with a current event, even if it's as mundane as going to the mall for a stroll and a cup of coffee and some Danish.

- Establish a "blues" fund. From time to time, and through circumstances beyond your control, things are going to go awry. Keep a candy jar in the cupboard with some mad money in it. Sometimes a nice dinner out with friends can raise the lowest of spirits.

Keep in mind that there are going to be low days in retirement, but strive for the high points, those "living for today and tomorrow" points that give meaning to your existence.

Always remember that when one door closes, another opens. Don't be afraid to step over the threshold to a new adventure.

41

TINY TRIUMPHS, SIMPLE PLEASURES ARE RETIREMENT BLESSINGS

Hark back to the first days of your marriage, when everything was new and splendid even if it was old and really not so grand. Remember the pine chest, battered and rickety, you two brought home from the junk store? It cost all of $2 back then, and the fun you had refinishing it and finding just the right knobs was worth millions.

You probably still have that pine chest, and newcomers to your home exclaim over the valuable antique you've no doubt inherited from some long-dead ancestor. You two smile at each other and remember the days.

When you were first married, it was easy to make memories from the simplest of pleasures. Now, after decades of marriage, it's not so easy. You and your spouse have eased into a routine in which much is taken for granted. In today's world, those tiny triumphs and simple pleasures of yesterday have too often been replaced by unrealistic goals, grueling challenges and materialistic achievements.

It is up to you two to make retirement as grand as was your new married life together. Look upon retirement as the newest stage of your married life, another honeymoon, if you will. Go back to the basics of life and recapture the thrill of those first few years. What matter if your hair's turned gray and there's a twinge of arthritis here and there?

Now with hours and hours of luxurious spare time stretching ahead of you both, it is time to recover the joy of life, and it certainly doesn't take a cruise to the Bahamas to do it.

Three couples tell how they've enriched their lives with tiny triumphs and simple pleasures by endowing creative chores with the trappings of significant accomplishments:

- Marlon and Louise are a fun-loving couple in their sixties who embellish even mundane chores with the fuss of a celebration. After these two freshened up their living room with a different color paint, they invited two other couples for a soup supper to view the results. The admiration of the paint job lasted only a few minutes, but the rest of the memorable evening was spent in a hilarious game of "Pictionary," amid plans for more such spontaneous "Job Well Done" parties.

- A trip to the past can provide a future. Norma is of British ancestry. After painstakingly researching her family back to sixteenth-century Kent, she decided that an English garden complete with herbal border was on her agenda. The library provided her with ideas. Her husband went right along with the plan, helping her dig, plant, and mulch. Little forays out to a nearby creek bed provided them with stones for their rockery. Their English garden may never be done—they are constantly adding and subtracting—but each act, no matter how small, is a triumph.

- Gearing down was a problem for Alexia, who, after many years in the fast lane of advertising, met and married Bob, a terrific fellow with a big sense of humor and an adequate but small retirement check. Used to the perks and pleasures of fast-lane living,

Alexia began to go quietly mad when the two retired to Bob's small home in the suburbs.

"I guess the turnaround of my life came the day I got up with absolutely nothing to do. Bob had an errand to run to a nearby hardware store, so I asked him to drop me at the library. Trade journals and up-style magazines, all fast reads, had been the extent of my literary adventures before I retired. I'd never had time to browse in our city's excellent library.

"To my amazement, I—the sophisticate, or so I thought—was like a kid in a candy store. There were zillions of books I had never had time to read. I was so excited I didn't know where to start, so I asked the librarian for ideas. Our particular library has a Great Books program. You read the books from the list; then check to see when that particular book's study group meets. She started me out with the classics. I hadn't opened one since they were crammed down my throat in college.

"If you'd told me two years ago I could get so excited about checking a book out of a library, I would have laughed. Small pleasures? I've found mine!"

Here are several other simple pleasures mentioned by retired couples who have relearned how to enjoy life:

- Clip grocery coupons, toss your savings into a jar and in six months count your loot. Enough for a night on the town? Enjoy.
- Walk. Although our walkways may not rival the footpaths of the English countryside, more and more cities are creating places where walking is a pleasure, not a hassle. You may be a heads-up walker bent on physical reward, but even more fun is a stroll with a loved one, enjoying the satisfaction of ever-changing sights and seasons.

- Take advantage of your retired years by enjoying such simple pleasures as visiting the zoo or a museum, going to the beach or a park for a picnic, taking up birdwatching, checking out flea markets, gardening, hiking or biking. Never forget that enormous pleasure can come from thinking small.

42

LIVING ONLY FOR EACH OTHER? THIS COULD BE DANGEROUS

Let me tell you the story of Inez and Richard. They'd met at the end of World War II. Both had been wed before. They met in an explosion of love and were married one week later and took off for the Air Force base where Richard was stationed. Her daughter remained behind with Inez's parents.

Inez and Richard spent the rest of his Air Force years at various bases throughout the world, with her daughter and eventually her daughter and children visiting intermittently. When Richard retired early from the service, they moved to a beautiful West Coast city, where they rented a lovely apartment high atop a hill.

And there they spent 35 years adoring each other to the exclusion of family. They both took second jobs, but at the end on the day hurried home to their little nest in the ivory tower. Eventually they retired for the second time and rejoiced in having all this time together. Oh, they visited with Inez's daughter and her children, but never more than once a year, although they lived less than 600 miles apart.

They chatted with other residents of the complex, but at no time did either of them seek outside interests, outside recreation, or outside friends.

They were a completely devoted couple, still baby-talking each other after 41 years of marriage and still very much in love. What a perfect couple, said everyone in their apartment house.

Sounds like a retirement paradise, doesn't it? So what's wrong with this picture?

Death inevitably came to one of them—Richard. And there Inez sat in her beautiful apartment, alone and crying. Their perfect retirement scenario had become a perfect hell.

Finally, Inez moved to the city where her daughter and grandchildren lived and, this time, began to live just for them—a course of action which drove her daughter nearly wild with frustration when she recognized the manipulative actions of this woman who was determined that her daughter's family should replace her Richard as the center of her universe.

Inez and Richard's problem, as a counselor I interviewed sees it, was that, during their service life, their social life was built in for them. When they returned to civilian life they had lost their social skills at initiating friendships and recreation, and did not work to regain them.

You and your loved one are retired and rejoicing in each other's company? That is perfectly wonderful, but never forget that there is life outside your circle of two.

You two should form new and wider bases of friendship, lest you end up like Inez and Richard, completely insulated and isolated from the world around them. Moving out into the world and creating new and different situations will never take away from the deep love you share with your mate; it will only enhance your fascination for each other. How can you both share yourself with the world? Some suggestions:

- Join an organization. If you haven't been joiners, now's the time to start. See Key 38 for how to get started.
- Attend a church, temple or other house of worship. Haven't been to one since childhood? You'll be amazed at how broad the religious experience has

154

become. There are houses of worship for every belief. Don't be averse to "church shopping." Sometimes you need the different experiences to see exactly what it is you require and can expect from a religion or belief. Finding the right one will give you an opportunity to meet friendly people who share your interests and beliefs.

- Get out and visit some place new at least once a week, and ask some new friends to go along. It may be only a drive to a new restaurant across town to use a "two-for-one" coupon cut from a shopper, but do something different.
- Don't do everything in tandem. Maybe your husband will opt for a men's service club or lodge. Maybe you'll choose the hospital auxiliary. Or maybe you'll join his club's women's auxiliary. In that event, you'll still share the same interests, but you both will be meeting new people.

As a wife, it may be up to you to get things moving in new directions, but I guarantee that if you try one or all of these suggestions for broadening your horizons, you're going to be amazed at how much depth you've added to your life together.

43

TWO HAPPILY RETIRED MEN OFFER ADVICE

What do retired men think about life after work? Two articulate and introspective men who have made their way through the first year of their retirement look back upon this period.

Ralph is a former administrator at a hospital. George is former state assistant director of transportation.

Each had his own way of dealing with retirement, and although their economic status may be higher than many retirees, their advice is sound and helpful no matter what the income.

Ralph's life has taken a new direction. He and his wife, Millie, discussed whether they would remain in the city where they'd lived for many years or move to a larger city nearby. They opted for the more urban environment.

"Moving to a big city didn't frighten us. We are both interested in cultural activities, and in the larger city we enjoy museums, galleries, exhibits and plays that are available on a daily basis."

Retirement is very satisfactory for Ralph, who has led an extremely active work life. His life now is divided between family, friends and his favorite activity, writing.

He offers this advice to wives helping their husbands toward a contented retired life:

- Don't let him be tied to time as you have always known it. A man may have his routines, but they don't have be be structured to the old work hours. Retirement is not an 8-to-5 job.

- Don't let him take on too many activities in order to fill up his empty hours. You may become so distracted by the dizzying pace that you may miss a signal pointing toward a new and exciting direction.
- Do together those things you rarely had time to do. "We go to movie matinees," says Ralph. "We had never had time to do that. We make it fun and spontaneous—just pick up and go. Marvelous!"
- Discuss seriously where you want to live. A change may be in order. In their new big city life, Ralph says there is never time to get bored.
- Maintain old friendships, but never be afraid to make new ones especially with younger people.
- Keep your mind open to new and exciting experiences and don't neglect your intellectual life. You may not have had time for cultural experiences while you were working. Now's the time to keep your eyes and your options open.

At first a bit wary of leaving his employment, George offers these tips to the wives:
- Be patient and let him lounge around a bit after retirement, but do help him get a routine of sorts. "Waking up in the morning and not knowing what you're going to do is scary stuff. Routines are wonderful, even if you establish one only to break it," George says.
- Help him toward exercising both his body and his mind. George maintains that walking is good for the body and the soul. "Walking has helped me take off weight, too, and that's a plus," he said.
- Wake up to the world. Have your second cup of coffee watching CNN or C-Span. The workings of government on C-Span afford a new outlook on the world around you, George said.

Both men agree that a loving and supportive wife is one of the most important keys to coping with retirement.

44

LOVE AND UNDERSTANDING SMOOTH OUT THE ROUGH SPOTS

You and your mate are doing pretty well in retirement, then whoops! Something sets you both off and you're really growling at each other. How can you smooth over those rough spots without relinquishing your own self-esteem and dignity?

First, let's define the problems. Usually, they are very basic, and once you identify the root cause, you can put the "smoothers" into practice.

ARE YOU REALLY LISTENING? Here's a dilly of a fight between two ordinarily sane people. They're sitting watching television one night and she says, "Oh, my legs are getting bad again." The husband, eyes and ears glued to the NBA finals, agrees: "Yes, I noticed last night when we were getting ready for bed that you're putting on weight and your legs are getting fatter."

The silence before her scream was icy; the scream, piercing. "Are you saying my legs are fat? I was talking about the rash on my ankles. And that's the last time I take off my clothes in front of you."

There was shouting, there was weeping. The situation really became ugly until, they both started to see the humor of the thing and began laughing.

No, I did not make this up. Even my imagination

couldn't come up with such a dumb fight. It happened exactly as I reported.

Could this have been avoided? Each partner should try to listen to what the other is saying, and when voicing feelings, should behave as a loving partner, not as a nagging parent.

MIXED SIGNALS: He was waiting on Corner A; she was waiting, laden with packages, on Corner B. When finally they got together, the traditional marital blaming scene began—I don't need to repeat the complaints, we've all lived through them.

Heading off this rough spot: In addition to really listening, as in the above hint, try "mirroring," that technique of repeating back to your partner what you think he is telling you. I don't know the percentages, but would be willing to bet that a plan is "heard" wrong about six times out of ten.

Smoothing it out: Refuse to be drawn into a pitched battle. Say quietly, "I think we got our signals mixed. Let's talk about it when we're calmer."

YOU ALWAYS...: This is a common problem among couples of all ages. The argument begins over one thing, and before you know it, it's gotten personal and that demon phrase "You always..." has crept in. That's when the infighting gets lethal.

Avoiding: If you can't head off an argument before it begins—always the best plan—have the decency to stick to the point at hand. Don't get personal and fight dirty by throwing past sins at your mate.

If he insists on arguing, and you feel that you are being badgered, simply say: "Fight fair. This appears to me to be a single-issue problem, and if you're going to get off the track I refuse to listen."

LA-LA LAND: If things have been going along smoothly, or so you thought, and then your mate comes up with an off-the-wall suggestion such as making what you consider an unnecessary purchase, don't shout: "You've got to be kidding. That's the dumbest thing I ever heard." Listen quietly and say: "My, that is interesting, but it's something we have to think about carefully. Can we put it on hold and talk about it again in several days?" Hopefully, by then he will have forgotten about it or if not, you will have your rebuttal carefully and sensibly planned.

SULKERS: Just as wildly frustrating as a screamer is a sulker who won't tell you what's wrong—just mopes around with lower lip stuck out, challenging you like a child to "Guess what's wrong!"

Never-fail remedy: Corner him and say, "I have no idea what is bugging you, but I refuse to be baited. If you won't discuss it, then I will never bring it up again. I won't play this game, so all your drama is wasted on me. Let's save time and talk, honey."

If he won't talk, then live up to your threat and go quietly about your business. It is no longer your problem.

These most common problem-causers can produce disruptions in any should-be-happy retirement. Sensible negotiations can usually heal the breach.

Some last hints:

- Think before you speak. An "open mouth, insert foot" boo-boo can hurt your mate.
- Be kind to one another. If you can't think of something nice to say, don't say anything. Criticism, even if richly deserved, is never easy to accept.
- If he shouts, be very quiet. It's unnerving to a shouter to have a mate listening and looking intently. "I do this with Bill," said Kay. "My quietness makes him feel uneasy. I think it makes him feel as if I'm making a mental list of 'get evens.' "

- If he's a door-slammer and a leaver, don't give him the satisfaction of racing after him with threats or pleas. Let him go.

Most marital squabbles do not reach monumental proportions so remain calm, keep the communication lines open if he chooses to communicate, and when it's over, seal your negotiations with a kiss.

45

AN INDEPENDENT WOMAN? NEGOTIATING WILL KEEP YOU FREE

Independence, that state of being free from the influence, control or determination of others, is a universally sought-after quality. While independence within a relationship is certainly desirable, in the sense that each person should be allowed the right to certain freedoms, there is, if the relationship is to flourish, the responsibility to adhere, within reason, to a partner's wishes. And this is where trouble can arise after retirement, because the prospect of a full-time husband may dismay a woman who is striving to achieve or maintain her hard-won independence.

Here's how Frances handled her life when Frank took an early retirement. She came late into independence. After being a traditional homemaker and mother for 30 years, she went back to college in her early fifties. After five tough years, she received her degree in social work, and by the time she was 60 had earned a master's degree and was working as a counselor. Six months after she began work, Frank was asked to take early retirement at 62. He was delighted. The couple's finances were in good shape and he had grand plans to buy a condo on the ocean and settle down to some serious boating and fishing.

His wife was not ready to be tied down to one spot. She told Frank, "I'm not ready. I stayed home with the children while you traveled around the country. Now, it's my turn. I want to live in different places, preferably with warm climates. While I work at my chosen profession, you can do whatever best suits you."

Now, after five years of Frances's plan for retirement, the couple has lived in three different locations: the Oregon coast, where Frank bought and renovated three condominiums, while Frances worked as a counselor to disturbed children; Honolulu, where she again did social work, while he refitted and refinished a boat for a friend; and the South Pacific where they both are currently working on a hospital ship. Frank, because of his railroad training, is employed in the engine room. Frances is the purser.

Frances pursued her dream of independence and turned it into reality. Frank was at first shocked at her declaration of independence; then as he began to think about it, he, a fair man, decided it would work. "I never know what she's going to do next," he said, adding that he greatly respects his wife.

For the woman who wants to achieve or maintain independence after a spouse's retirement, one retirement counselor has this advice:

There are husbands who, because of retirement, suffer a loss of self-esteem. Therefore, a wife desiring her own life should be gentle when broaching the subject of "her turn." It is possible to state your needs without overwhelming a mate who has assumed that his wife will always be the same person. Also, not all husbands are as open to change as was Frank.

"A husband's ego is a fragile thing," the counselor says, "and if a wife doesn't intend to be there to perform all the services she has in the past, she should reassure him that she will be there with emotional support."

Another counselor recommends that women go on the assertive, not the aggressive, when maintaining their independence. Assertiveness behavior is positive and rewarding action, she says.

163

Here are tips for achieving or retaining independence after retirement:

- If a complete change of pace is what you desire, go easy into the marital arena. Don't hit a husband with the shotgun approach of "I am going to do this, and this, and this." Realistically think through your goals based on your financial and emotional capability. Then, as did Frances, approach him rationally with a plan that he can understand without feeling threatened. Appeal, without pleading, to him through his sense of fairness.
- After you've quietly but firmly outlined your wishes, give him the opportunity to outline his thoughts.
- Establish a special time, whether it's morning or afternoon or evening, that is "your" time. If there are objections, using the quiet/firm tactic again, say "This is my time and I shall spend it as I choose to spend it."
- If there is the one-car problem in your household, work out your schedule on a weekly basis ahead of time so you won't be left without wheels when you need them. One couple worked out a "mornings the car is his, afternoons it's mine" schedule. This may be too inflexible for many, but it works for them.

Do not allow yourself to be manipulated or outmaneuvered on your period of time, and do not allow any comments or questions such as "Well, what did you get accomplished today?" dismay you. Your time is your time, and if you choose to spend it smelling the roses, that's your choice as an independent woman.

46

A SPECIAL PROBLEM: DRINKING

You and your mate have been married for a long time. Through the years you two have done a bit of social drinking, but never to excess. You were too caught up in the business of life and all that that entails: children, work, home.

As mentioned before, your role as a wife may not change that much when your husband comes home to stay. You have your household duties and pleasures. He's the one with empty hours to fill, and that may initiate a problem you never thought you'd have to face—he's drinking too much.

A not very worldly woman, Greta realized that her husband, Al, was having trouble adjusting to retirement. He spent far too much time on the sofa dozing, and when he wasn't dozing, he was puttering around in the garage doing something or other. He was not, she realized, a happy man, but she never thought of alcohol until she went to look for a hammer in the tool cabinet.

When she opened the door, empty vodka bottles, lots of them, began rolling out.

"I sat down and began to cry. It was the last thing in the world I suspected. He'd never acted the way I thought a drunk acted, but what do I know about a drunk except the comic ones I see on TV?"

In a February 1991 article in the American Association of Retired Persons (AARP) "Bulletin," a report from the Mayo Clinic in Rochester, Minnesota, states that as many as 10 percent of the 42 million Americans age 60 and older "are problem drinkers."

The article goes on to say that the percentage may be even higher, because alcohol abuse in older people is often underdiagnosed and underreported.

A growing number of those folks are heretofore social drinkers who have increased their alcohol intake after age sixty. According to the AARP "Bulletin" the 1988 Mayo Clinic study discovered that 41 percent of persons age 65 and older who enrolled in the clinic's alcoholism treatment program first reported symptoms of alcoholism after age 60.

Theories on causes range from boredom, because of more leisure time, to the pressures of retirement, the latter problem more prevalent in men.

How can you you tell if your husband is using alcohol as therapy against a perhaps unwanted and frightening retirement?

In the AARP "Bulletin" report, the National Institute on Alcohol Abuse and Alcoholism offers these warning signs:

—Mood swings such as breaking into tears or becoming hostile.

—Short-term memory loss.

—Loss of appetite.

—Untidy or unclean personal appearance.

—Apparent immunity to prescribed medications.

—Repeated falls, cuts, bruises, burns from smoking.

—Loss of interest in family, hobbies or friends.

Let's hope this isn't a situation you'll face after retirement, but if you suspect that alcoholism is a problem with your loved one, confide your suspicions to your family physician or religious counselor. He or she will be able to offer suggestions on where to begin.

The AARP "Bulletin" reports that Alcoholics Anonymous has created special Golden Years groups in some areas. Women for Sobriety, another national self-help group, also has local chapters.

Your faith, love, and support can be of great help in the recovery process, because therapy works well for those individuals able to stick to it. In the AARP "Bulletin" article, Dr. Sheldon Zimberg, psychiatrist at the Mount Sinai School of Medicine in New York, says, "Older alcohol-dependent people are not beyond help. They normally respond well to therapy if we can get them into a treatment program."

47

POSTRETIREMENT EMPLOYMENT? WHY NOT?

Although a couple can do much in the way of planning the Big Picture of retirement, it is not possible to forecast a day-by-day retirement routine.

"Retirement is definitely an on-the-job training situation, and some people are not really ready to retire. They like what they're doing and remember, work is only work when you'd rather be doing something else," says a recent retiree. "When a man has retired because of policy, not desire, and is still full of energy and wants to continue being a useful and contributing person, he may want to go back to work."

In fact, as one of the retirement counselors I interviewed suggests, some people should never retire. Their mental and physical health and welfare are tied to productive employment.

A retired Episcopal minister, who claims he is a typical Type-A personality, said his is a profession in which a person does not stop being what he was at the time of mandatory retirement. Once a minister, always a minister, he says. He retired from the ministry one week, and went back to work the following week as a part-time hospital chaplain, a job he finds most satisfying.

His wife, Barbara, was definitely a part of this second-vocation choice, because a decision such as this will not work unless certain commitments are made between husband and wife, he said.

Arthur was another Type-A fireball who was eased back into the work world by his wife, Carrie. He had been retired only six weeks when Carrie realized that it might be wise for her hitherto active husband, owner of a trucking firm, to get back into the harness.

"If women of today still wrung their hands helplessly in despair, I would have been doing it," says Carrie, who herself is a busy-bee of a woman. "We were driving each other crazy. Arthur started one project a day, and if it was possible to finish that project in a day, he did it. He'd work in the garage clear into the night. He was obsessed with the challenge of accomplishment. I think it was a self-proof thing. I saw more of him when he was working."

Arthur had been owner/manager of a trucking firm he'd built up from one truck hauling lumber to construction sites. When he reached 62, he retired to accommodate his son, who was as full of energy as his father and was champing at the bit to try out new ideas.

"It hurt my feelings that life with me wasn't enough for him, but I do love him. It nearly made me cry to see Arthur looking as if life were just about over," says Carrie. "There are only so many jobs you can do around the house."

A born Miss Fix-It, Carrie began looking in the help-wanted ads of the local paper. One day she found a job exactly cut out for a man of Arthur's talents. A small trucking firm needed a part-time dispatcher. That night at dinner, she casually showed him the ad. The next morning, he applied and was hired. Now he works 20 hours a week and wakes up each morning in a happy frame of mind. He is a new man, and Carrie is a contented woman because her sweetheart has a new purpose in life.

Key 33 discusses some escape routes for a wife if retired life becomes too much. Taking a job after retirement is an escape route that many wives choose rather than taking up a hobby.

If you or your husband decides that one or the other of you would benefit from a second vocation, here are several decision-making tips offered by some experts in the retirement field:

- If possible, make your second retirement job one that offers you flexibility in work hours, so that you have time to spend with your mate and your family.
- Unless you're a person who thrives on heavy competition, don't take on a job where you are the key player.
- Look for a position where you learn new skills but have the opportunity to use and enlarge the skills you already have. "Taking the part of work you most enjoyed in your previous employment and building on this experience is a fine way to enter the work world again. If you have to take some classes to increase your expertise, this can be very stimulating and beneficial to a retired person," says a retirement planning instructor.
- "A part-time situation where you still have time to enjoy retirement may be the answer," says another counselor.
- Take a job that is a fairly routine work situation. Don't take on one that calls for high risk taking unless you have the temperament and stamina to accept the risks involved.

Although a second vocation after the first may not be for everyone, it is quite often the answer for many couples. Unless there is a pressing financial need, a postretirement job should be for fun, stimulation and enrichment—and remember, when it isn't fun anymore, you can walk away from it!

48

"FOR BETTER OR WORSE"—BUT HOW MUCH WORSE?

What is acceptable or not acceptable behavior within a marriage differs from wife to wife. What could be considered standard behavior tolerated with fortitude, even good humor, by an "old wife" may be less than favorably received by a "new wife." A lot of elements go into making up a relationship, even one that appears to be filled with hostility.

King and Patti had been married, in her words, "forever." She was a teen-ager barely out of high school when they were wed. In two years, Patti began having babies, something you did in the 1950s without much planning and very little prevention.

A talented and handsome fellow, King soon began to chafe under the bonds of matrimony, but his basic decency kept him from divorcing, even though his temper made life with him nigh unbearable.

One cold evening in January, shortly after King's retirement, the couple awoke to the ominous sounds of gurgling in the shower. A pipe had frozen, and backed-up sludge was filling the shower stall at a frightening rate. King barked orders, and Patti leaped to obey, but not fast enough.

"Within one minute our marriage was over," said Patti, who had lived through 38 years of divorce threats, near-abandonment and verbal abuse. "He screamed curses at my stupidity so violently that he fell to the floor and couldn't breathe. He'd cursed all his life and

I'd put up with it, but this time I realized that there might come a day when he could die before my very eyes and with a curse on his lips."

She packed her bags the next morning and left the marriage for good.

"What did I do?" asked a bewildered King. "I wasn't any different than I've ever been."

The answer was simple: Patti had reached her limit of wifely endurance. The reason she had stayed so long was equally simple: "I loved him."

She divorced him and eventually made a wonderful late-life marriage, but she still cherishes memories of King.

"We shared our youth and our dreams. There were good times. You don't forget that, but I knew I had to get out for my own sanity."

Yes, even in retirement, marriages do fail. It is not a happy subject to write about, but it is reality.

King's churlish intimidation of Patti had been part of their relationship, one which she accepted for years. Perhaps your husband has been an easygoing guy most of your married life, but suddenly he turns into the husband from hell. What's going on?

Could it be:

—Physical? Is there some illness of which you haven't been aware? Many folks will keep going, keep pushing themselves until there is no longer a reason to push, then fall ill. Make an appointment and get him to a physician, and sit right there with him during the visit. Physicians are not required to divulge diagnoses or discussions even to a wife. Best to be right there.

—Postretirement depression? Mood swings are frequent as a man wrestles with the fact that he is no longer young. He has to take out his anger and frustration on someone, and his wife is closest at hand. This is an unfair situation, and only you will know how much of this nonsense you're going to stand.

—Insecurity? To regain control of their lives after retirement, men have been known to revert to cruel behavior to the one who loves them best. This can be manifested through verbal abuse, irrational jealousy or, even worse, physical abuse.

There is no pat answer as to when or whether you should leave a husband whose behavior is intolerable, except in a case of physical abuse. In that situation, there is absolutely no reason to stay with a man who batters you.

However, if his problem is emotional and a solution may be possible, take into account Ann Landers' sage question: "Am I better off with or without this man?"

If you feel you're better off with your husband, no matter how offensive he's become, then take steps to improve your position. After you get him to a doctor and understand the situation, it's often wise to hie yourself to a counselor. Counselors don't always advise; they simply help a person come to terms with the situation, then aid the person in finding the keys to cope.

If you make the decision to leave, then hire a good lawyer and don't look back. If your spouse has chosen to ruin the rest of his life, there is absolutely no reason to stay and let him pull you down with him.

49

DANGER SIGNALS: WHEN ALL IS NOT RIGHT

"Many men develop physical and psychological problems after retirement, but most of these problems routinely disappear after a period of adjustment," said one personal counselor, who added, "However, some men are so wrapped up in their workplace that they feel upon leaving it they have lost their reason for living."

So let's say you've read this book and tried most of the suggestions offered by wives, but still all is not right. You have reassured your mate of your love and devotion and supported the part of his life that remains healthy, but still he languishes. As a wife you know your husband's behavior patterns, and you realize that the depression over leaving the workplace has lasted much longer than is healthy.

A counselor offers this advice for detecting serious depression:

- He lacks zest for life, often manifested by unwillingness to participate in any outside activity.
- He develops a reclusive personality and withdraws when guests, even family members, appear on the scene.
- He shows lack of care for self. This can be evident in grooming. If he doesn't want to shave for several days, don't be concerned. However, if he gives up shaving and bathing for a period of time, this is not mentally healthy.
- He develops peculiar eating patterns, such as eating too much or too little, or adopting strange food fads.

- His sleeping habits are erratic. They may range from sleeping too much to sleeping too little.
- He has no desire to participate in any recreation.
- He becomes overwhelmingly conscious of his body's disorders and blows up any minor ailment into a terminal disease.
- His sex drive fails. If he is impotent, this may be a physical problem due to age, and can often be helped. If a physical cause is ruled out, then the lack of sex drive could be the result of depression.
- He talks of "life being over" or "What's the use?" or "ending it all." Talk of suicide is frightening, and it is not true that people who talk of suicide rarely try it. They do.
- He has mood swings ranging from silence to violent temper outbursts.

All right. You have decided something is terribly wrong. What do you do about it?

- Coax him to visit the family doctor. This is not always easy to do, but try very hard to convince him that this visit is for your peace of mind. Concern for you, his wife, will often get him up and moving to a physician.
- If you cannot get Mohammed to the mountain, try to get the mountain to Mohammed. In this day and age, a doctor making a house call is as rare as a free lunch, but visit your family physician yourself and outline the symptoms. Impress upon the doctor the seriousness of the situation.
- If you are unable to persuade a doctor to visit, get in touch with your local Health Department and describe the problem. In many states, there are visiting nurse practitioners who can come to the home and make a simple diagnosis.
- If the diagnosis is made that he does indeed need help and you still can't get him up and moving, call on a

family member or good friend. If necessary, call your husband's former place of employment and ask to speak to the personnel representative if there is one. Company personnel often are knowledgeable about services available. Call your minister or rabbi and ask for aid. These people do make house calls and are trained to offer assistance in this kind of situation.

This will be an extremely traumatic time for you, but you should never let yourself feel guilty about your husband's behavior. The problem may be yours to share with him, but don't assume the blame for what is happening to him. Clinical depression is a condition that is deep within the person who is suffering from it.

50

THE 10 MOST IMPORTANT KEYS TO LIVING WITH A RETIRED HUSBAND

In the previous 49 keys, I have attempted to discuss as many scenarios as possible that a wife will encounter as she and her husband head into their retirement years.

In reviewing these scenarios and resultant interviews with professionals in the field and with wives of retired husbands, it appears that there are 10 basic keys to coping with the problems that might arise.

If you love this man and want your retirement together to be the best it can be, always remember to:

1. Live as much as possible in the present moment with your love. There are times for nostalgia and remembrances of things past, but the majority of your life together should be built on the here and now, and the tomorrow. Don't be afraid to try the new and different, because making memories today for tomorrow should be your watchword.

2. Learn to communicate, and never forget that communication is as much listening as it is talking. Encourage your husband to speak by listening to every word he says, making sure you let him get his thought out before you leap in to finish it for him.

3. Keep your sense of humor close at hand at all times. A witty comment and a giggle can help

keep anger, despair, even the world itself at a distance.

4. Take care of yourself while you're taking care of him. Don't let yourself be exploited. You are just as important a person as is your retired husband and never forget it.

5. Keep accusatory statements out of your tone and out of your life. Questions and statements beginning with "Why did you...?" and "Why do you always...?" and "You never..." are particularly destructive to a marriage. Never, even in the height of a quarrel, drag up hurtful experiences of the past. This is today.

6. Be as polite and gentle to your mate as you would to a person whom you're trying to impress. A fed-up wife once said, "All I ask is that you be as nice to me as you are to a customer."

7. Assess yourself and your relationship with your mate to ascertain whether you have been fair and open with each other and are meeting each other's needs. If there are problems, work at solving them together.

8. View your husband as the man you married, and never lose sight of what attracted you to him in the first place. Remind him of those endearing traits often. Remember that the inner man of your man needs constant and loving strokes.

9. Keep your husband comfortable, respected and desired. Men whose wives provide these three essentials are lucky indeed.

10. These are your golden years—a sentimental way of putting it but nonetheless the truth—so do not waste them.

QUESTIONS AND ANSWERS

What's going to happen now? Will we be happy? What should we expect?

These are the questions most asked by wives whose husbands are facing retirement, but these three questions are only the tip of the retirement iceberg. There are many other questions asked by wives concerned about the life ahead. We'll touch on a few of them here.

But first, let's tackle the Big Three:

Q. What's going to happen now?
A. The answer begins with another question. What do you want to happen now? If you say that you want things to be the same as they have been, you're going to be disappointed. This is another phase of your life together, and you should treat it as such. Don't be afraid. Be willing to open your eyes, your hearts, and your minds to fresh and different experiences. New beginnings can be fun.

Q. Will we be happy?
A. Life does not come with guarantees. But if you and your mate set out with a positive attitude, there's a very good chance you will both find joy and contentment. Appreciating today rather than mourning yesterday or rushing for tomorrow is important, because, too often, we are so busy racing toward one destination that we fail to appreciate the journey.

Q. What should we expect?

A. Let's have one contented wife answer that question: "Look upon retirement as another honeymoon. It's similar to the first because you are two individuals setting out on a new adventure and getting to know each other in a different setting. Sure, there are going to be some trouble spots, but if you use a lot of common sense, patience and love, it's going to be just fine."

Q. Is pre-retirement planning in areas other than financial matters a must?

A. Certainly you'll be able to manage if you and your mate don't participate in a retirement planning session, but if you do, it may be much easier. Counselors touch on subjects such as living arrangements, typical problems you may encounter and how to improve the quality of your life with meaningful activities. The directors say no session is conducted without at least one couple making amazing discoveries about each other's retirement goals.

Q. We've lived together but apart for years. He's been out in the working world, while I've preferred to stay home. Are we going to have anything in common now?

A. If you've been married for many years, you've obviously shared a variety of experiences. Now is the time to build upon these to achieve a more balanced lifestyle together. If you've been married just a short time, retirement is a wonderful time to explore and discover new facets of your relationship.

Q. Will our marriage remain on an even keel if I continue with my career, which I love?

A. You may have to compartmentalize your work activities for a period of time while you are helping your husband get settled in retirement, but by using patience, compassion, love and understanding, there is no reason you can not continue with your career while enjoying marital contentment.

Q. I have my house and my life arranged very neatly. Will we be in each other's way?
A. When you speak of "my" house and "my" life, don't forget that it's *his* house, also, and that *his* life is involved here as well. Territorial strife, as I call it, can be resolved if you work together to make your mutual space comfortable for both of you. Maintaining your own independence and individual lifestyle may take some compromises and concessions, but if you aid your mate in finding new purpose in his new life, you both will benefit.

Q. My husband has never had a hobby. How can I help him find one?
A. "Help him" is the key phrase here. Don't try to force a hobby on a husband; let him choose his own. However, you can steer him in the right direction by paying close attention to what interests him, then helping him find an outlet for his interest. Don't neglect volunteering, which is fast becoming a way of life for many retired people, because helping someone or helping them help themselves is a most rewarding activity.

Q. Can I expect more help around the house?
A. Certainly, you can, so don't be afraid to ask for it. However, make your needs known in a calm and rational way because demanding rarely produces the desired results. Remember, retirement is a partnership right down to cleaning the shower stall and dusting Grandma's china.

Q. Does the end of our work life mean the end of our sex life?

A. It shouldn't, if you are in good health. You will have more time and be more relaxed, so sex can be as much fun as ever—even more so, if you're willing to experiment!

Q. What is the most important ingredient in a successful retirement?

A. The same ingredient responsible for any successful relationship: communication. If you and your husband can speak openly about your needs and feelings, there are few retirement problems that can't be solved.

INFORMATION GUIDE

The American Association of Retired Persons (AARP) is a national organization that can supply you with a wealth of information on most anything that has to do with retirement. If they do not have the information themselves, they can usually tell you where to find it.

The state agencies listed after the AARP are also excellent sources of information. Check with them about legal questions that fall within the state's province and to find out what types of services they offer for retired persons.

American Association of Retired Persons (AARP)
    Administrative offices: 1909 K Street NW
    Washington, DC 20049   (202) 872–4700

Alabama Commission on Aging
    770 Washington Avenue, Suite 470
    Montgomery, AL 36130   (205) 242–5743

Older Alaskans Commission
    P.O. Box C
    Juneau, AK 99811–0209   (907) 465–3250

Territorial Administration on Aging
    Government of American Samoa
    Pago Pago, AS 96799   (694) 633–1251

Aging and Adult Administration
  Department of Economic Security
  1400 West Washington
  Phoenix, AZ 85007   (800) 352–3792

Arkansas Department of Human Services
  Division of Aging and Adult Services
  Donaghey Building, Suite 1428
  Main and 7th Streets
  Little Rock, AR 72201   (501) 682–2441

California Department of Aging
  1600 K Street
  Sacramento, CA 95814   (916) 322–5290

Department of Social Services
  Aging and Adult Services
  1575 Sherman Street, Tenth Floor
  Denver, CO 80203–1714   (303) 866–5905

Department of Community and Cultural Affairs
  Civic Center
  Commonwealth of Northern Mariana Islands
  Saipan, CM 96950   (670) 234–6011

Connecticut Department on Aging
  175 Main Street
  Hartford, CT 06106   (800) 443–9946

Delaware Division of Aging
  Department of Health and Social Services
  1901 North Dupont Highway, Second Floor
  New Castle, DE 19720   (302) 421–6791

District of Columbia Office on Aging
  Executive Office of the Mayor
  1424 K Street, NW, Second Floor
  Washington, DC 20005   (202) 724–5622

Aging and Adult Services
  Department of Health and Rehabilitative Services
  1323 Winewood Boulevard, Building 2, Room 328
  Tallahassee, FL 32339–07009   (800) 342–0825

Department of Human Resources
  Office of Aging
  878 Peachtree Street, NE, Sixth Floor
  Atlanta, GA 30309   (404) 894–5333

Department of Public Health
  Division of Senior Citizens
  P.O. Box 2816
  Government of Guam
  Agana, GU 96910   (671) 734–2942

Hawaii Executive Office on Aging
  335 Merchant Street, Room 241
  Honolulu, HI 96813   (808) 548–2593

Idaho Office on Aging
  State House, Room 108
  Boise, ID 83720   (208) 334–3833

Illinois Department on Aging
  421 East Capitol Avenue
  Springfield, IL 62701   (800) 252–8966

Indiana Department of Human Services
  150 West Market Street
  P.O. Box 7083
  Indianapolis, IN 46207–7083   (800) 545–7763

Department of Elder Affairs
  Jewett Building, Suite 236
  914 Grand Avenue
  Des Moines, IA 50319   (515) 281–5187

Kansas Department on Aging
  Docking State Office Building
  915 S.W. Harrison
  Topeka, KS 66612–1500   (800) 432–3535

Division for Aging Services
  Cabinet for Human Resources
  275 East Main Street
  Frankfort, KY 40621   (502) 564–6930

Governor's Office of Elderly Affairs
  P.O. Box 80374
  Baton Rouge, LA 70898–0374   (504) 925–1700

Department for Human Services
  Bureau of Elder and Adult Services
  State House, Station 11
  35 Anthony Avenue
  Augusta, ME 04333   (207) 289–2561

Maryland Office on Aging
  301 West Preston Street
  Baltimore, MD 21201   (800) 338–0153

Massachusetts Executive Office of Elder Affairs
38 Chauncy Street
Boston, MA 02111   (800) 882–2003

Office of Services to the Aging
P.O. Box 30026
Lansing, MI 48909   (517) 373–8230

Minnesota Board on Aging
Human Services Building, Fourth Floor
444 Lafayette Road
St. Paul, MN 55155–3843   (612) 296–2770

Department of Human Services
Council on Aging
Division of Aging and Adult Services
421 West Pascagoula Street
Jackson, MS 39203   (800) 222–7622

Department of Social Services
Division of Aging
615 Howerton Court
P.O. Box 1337
Jefferson City, MO 65102   (314) 751–3082

Governor's Office of Aging
Capitol Station, Room 219
Helena, MT 59620   (800) 332–2272

Department on Aging
301 Centennial Mall South
P.O. Box 95044
Lincoln, NE 68509   (402) 471–2306

Division for Aging Services
  State Mail Room
  Las Vegas, NV 89158   (702) 486–3545

New Hampshire Department of
Health and Human Services
  Division of Elderly and Adult Services
  6 Hazen Drive
  Concord, NH 03301   (603) 271–4390

New Jersey Division on Aging
  Department of Community Affairs
  101 South Broad Street, CN 807
  Trenton, NJ 08625–0807   (800) 792–8820

New Mexico State Agency on Aging
  La Villa Rivera Building, Fourth Floor
  224 East Palace Avenue
  Santa Fe, NM 87501   (800) 432–2080

New York State Office for the Aging
  Agency Building #2
  Empire State Plaza
  Albany, NY 12223   (518) 474–5731

Department of Human Resources
  North Carolina Division of Aging
  693 Palmer Drive, Box 29531
  Raleigh, NC 27626–0531   (919) 733–3983

North Dakota Department of Human Services
  Aging Services Division
  State Capitol Building
  Bismarck, ND 58505   (701) 224–2577

Ohio Department of Aging
  50 West Broad Street, Eighth Floor
  Columbus, OH 43215   (614) 466–5500

Department of Human Services
  Aging Services Division
  P.O. Box 25352
  Oklahoma City, OK 73125   (405) 521–2327

Department of Human Resources
  Senior and Disabled Services Division
  313 Public Service Building
  Salem, OR 97310   (503) 378–4728

Department of Aging
  231 State Street (Barto Building)
  Harrisburg, PA 17101   (717) 783–1550

Puerto Rico Office of Elderly Affairs
  Call Box 50063
  Old San Juan Station, PR 00902

Department of Social Services
  State Agency on Aging
  Republic of Palau
  Koror, Palau, PL 96940

Department of Elderly Affairs
  160 Pine Street
  Providence, RI 02903   (800) 752–8088

South Carolina Commission on Aging
  400 Arbor Lake Drive
  Suite B–500
  Columbia, SC 29223   (800) 922–1107

Office of Adult Services and Aging
  Richard Kneip Building
  700 Governors Drive
  Pierre, SD 57501–4855   (605) 773–3656

Tennessee Commission on Aging
  706 Church Street, Suite 201
  Nashville, TN 37219–5573   (615) 741–2056

Texas Department on Aging
  P.O. Box 12786
  Capitol Station
  Austin, TX 78711   (512) 444–2727

Utah Division on Aging and Adult Services
  120 North 200 West, Room 4A
  P.O. Box 45500
  Salt Lake City, UT 84145–0500   (801) 538–3910

Department of Aging and Disabilities
  103 South Main Street
  Waterbury, VT 05676   (802) 241–2400

Virgin Islands Department of Human Services
  Barbel Plaza South
  Charlotte Amalie
  St. Thomas, VI 00802   (809) 774–0930

Virginia Department for the Aging
  700 East Franklin Street, Tenth Floor
  Richmond, VA 23219–2327   (800) 552–4464

Department of Social and Health Services
  Aging and Adult Services Administration
  Main Stop, OB–44–A
  Olympia, WA 98504   (800) 422–3263

West Virginia Commission on Aging
  State Capital Complex-Holly Grove
  1710 Kanawha Boulevard
  Charleston, WV 24305   (800) 642–3671

Department of Health and Social Services
  Bureau on Aging
  1 West Wilson Street, Room 480
  P.O. Box 7851
  Madison, WI 53707   (608) 266–2536

Commission on Aging
  Hathaway Building, First Floor
  Cheyenne, WY 82002   (307) 777–7986

BIBLIOGRAPHY

"Alcoholism and Seniors." *AARP Bulletin,* February 1991.

Bolles, Richard. *The Three Boxes of Life (And How to Get Out of Them).* Berkeley: Ten Speed Press, 1981.

Bradford, Leland P. and Martha I. Bradford. *Retirement: Coping with Emotional Upheavals.* Chicago: Nelson Hall, 1979.

Brody, Robert. "Getting Off Your Workday Treadmill." *50 Plus,* September 1988.

Butcher, Lee. *Retirement Without Fear.* Princeton: Dow Jones Books, 1978.

"Formula for Marital Longevity." *Modern Maturity,* June-July 1991.

Gill, Bettye and John Clyde. *Solving the Puzzlement of Retirement Planning (Designed to Help You Plan for Retirement).* Oregon Retirement Planning Services, Salem, Oregon, 1990.

Hatcher, Robert A., Dr. "Listening." A paper delivered at Georgia State University, May 1974.

Hemmings, Roy, editor. *65 Mistakes to Avoid in Retirement.* New York: Retirement Living Publishing Co., 1987.

Knopf, Olga, M.D. *Facts and Fallacies of Growing Old.* New York: Viking Press, 1975.

Leisure and Your Successful Retirement. New York: Retirement Living Publishing Co., 1988.

Phelps, Stanlee and Nancy Austin. *The Assertive Woman.* San Luis Obispo, California: Impact Publishers, 1987.

Rubin, Theodore Isaac, M.D. *Compassion and Self-Hate—Alternative to Despair.* New York: D. McKay Co., 1975.

Shank, Howard. *Management Retirement: The Surprising Opportunities and Challenges.* Chicago: Contemporary Books Inc., 1985.

Tannen, Deborah, Ph.D. "How to Break Talk Gridlock." *Self,* January 1991.

"10 Keys to Effective Listening." *Executive Female.* September-October 1980.

What I Wish Someone Had Told Me About Retirement. First Hand Personal Accounts. New York: Retirement Living Publishing Co., 1987.

INDEX

195